EP MAY 1976

KT-490-834

Summer of a Million Wings

ARCTIC QUEST FOR THE SEA EAGLE

Summer
of a Million Wings

ARCTIC QUEST FOR THE SEA EAGLE

Hugh Brandon-Cox

*Illustrated with photographs
and sketches by the author*

DAVID & CHARLES
NEWTON ABBOT

0 7153 6355 7

This book is dedicated to Ronald Johanssen,
without whose strong arms the expedition
would not have succeeded

Set in 12 on 13pt Bembo
and printed in Great Britain by
Latimer Trend & Company Ltd Plymouth
for David & Charles (Holdings) Limited
South Devon House Newton Abbot Devon

Contents

List of Plates

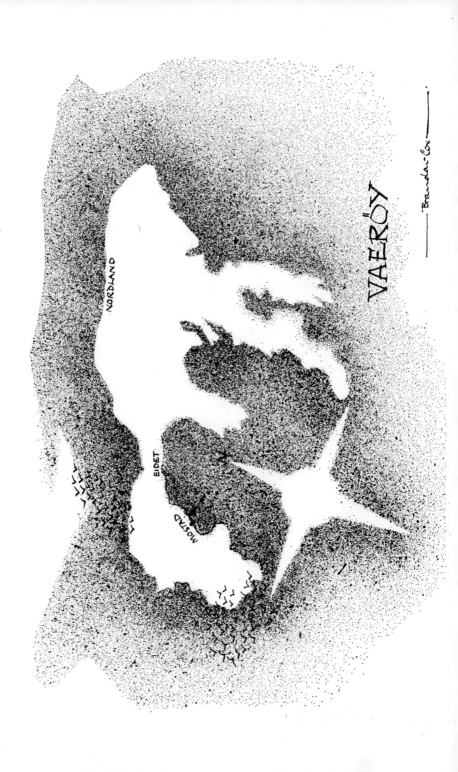

VAERØY

NORDLAND

EIDET

MOSTAD

Brundarlov

1 *Bastions of the North*

The evening of 20 August: the candle flame splutters fitfully whilst the shadows dance on the wooden walls of the room in the old neglected school-house at the edge of the sea in a deserted village in North Norway. The small building on its base of rocks groans and creaks as the shrieking wind howls in from the sea. The wind is mixed with dirty grey salt spray as it strikes against the window-panes.

Across the wide and stormy bay the mountains are obscured by thick grey clouds that swirl down almost to the level of the angry white-topped waves.

The sense of isolation is strong. Around the school-house are the boarded-up shells of the wooden houses, once filled with life, from which came the children to fill the large single classroom. Mostad, the village under the great cliff, now lives on its memories, inhabited by one lonely old man and his wife and the teeming millions of sea birds that sweep restlessly around the cliffs all summer.

The wildness of the late summer storm, a scene so common in this region above the Arctic Circle, affects the senses so that after a while we sit as if in a trance whilst the gloom in the small room grows deeper where the candle light does not reach.

9

Ulla-Maija, my Finnish companion, shakes herself from her reverie and turns to place more driftwood on the old black iron stove. In the oven the rye bread is rising and turning golden brown. When the door is opened for a moment for the baking to be controlled the room is filled with the strong sour odour of the bread. Wood for the fire has been gathered from the rocks on the tide-edge. The strength of the draught makes the grey wood draw into fierce flames of bright yellow.

The long days and nights of eternal light in the period of the midnight sun were over. Very soon the days would pass from their continual summer lightness to the pale twilight of winter. Sunless would be the long dark days that are little distinguishable from the nights.

Cliffs that had been filled with life all summer would soon grow cold and neglected. The flowers that had brightened them with a rainbow of colour would be replaced by a layer of snow over the slopes and the summits of the mountains. Only the deep echoing 'korp, korp' of a few ravens who remained faithful to their nesting cracks all winter, and the high circling sea eagles with their occasional high yelping cries, would give a semblance of life.

Outside the school-house on that gloomy late August evening there was little sound from the birds. Gale-force winds and the driving rain had silenced even their cries. The dull booming of waves pounding the rocks by the sea edge continued hour after hour. Thankfully we gathered closer to the fire. Summer seemed a long time ago.

On the nights when the weather had been kinder, from late in July until this storm weather held us prisoner, the clear air had been filled with the hideous gargling growls of the female guillemots and razorbills. Riding the waves of the bay some distance from the shore rocks, they had shouted encouragement to the young to follow them out to sea. There had been little chance of any sleep until well past midnight in those late evenings that were already feeling the breath of autumn. For centuries the bay had probably known these wild calls in late July. They are some of the strangest in nature.

Vertically rise the cliffs in all their splendour behind the school-house and along the whole length of the bay in which the deserted village is situated. Close to their summits are the ledges and cracks and tunnel-filled slopes so thickly populated by guillemots, razorbills and puffins in summer. From the rather terrifying heights of these ledges on which so many guillemots and razor-bills are hatched, the youngsters can look down on the sea far below.

When the colonies nest directly over the water then all is well. Even a long sloping fall will not harm the youngsters, who are strongly built and excellent swimmers as soon as they touch water. They have little to fear from their high leaps.

Along the precipitous cliffs rising as a solid wall behind Mostad, however, the nesting ledges are far from the sea. A wide expanse of rock and grass must be negotiated before the safety of the water is reached.

Probably because these high ledges are so difficult to approach and have always offered such good facilities to the birds and their eggs, they have been used for generations by the auks. But from the moment when the young birds must take their plunge into the unknown, they are no longer ideal sites.

Still quite small, although covered with youthful feathering resembling the parents, these little penguins of the northern world have as yet merely undeveloped wing-stumps from which the flight feathers have not grown. They are ill-prepared for the testing first flight into which they are urged and driven by the parents eager to be away out to sea.

The instinctive urge to leave the bird rocks and face the deep open waters free from predators in time for the autumn moult grows daily stronger as July passes and draws to a close.

On the high ledges, through the veils of mist and fog, the growl-ing grows louder and more aggressive. At last the parents cease to bring back the long silver fish on which the young have been fed.

Whether their single young are ready to face the open sea or not, they have to be forced into all too-early flight.

One after another the little auks have to be pushed or encouraged to leap from the safety of the shelf of rock which has been their world. Frantically whirring their small wings at great speed, they try to push their plump bodies as far as possible away from the cliff in company with their parents. Quickly the wings fail to hold them up, but acting as a kind of parachute the stumps break their fall to the rocks far below.

Remarkably the young birds, thudding on to the grass or the rocks with considerable force, usually manage to rise again. They shake their heads and commence to run on wide dark feet towards the anxious growls luring them on towards the sea. We felt a sense of irritation towards the parents, who just lay about 100 yards offshore from the boulders and growled with such sustained howls that it became difficult for us to hear each other speak at times.

It was not difficult to see the small black and white forms, walking and stumbling at a remarkable speed, uttering thin piping calls which made their discovery even easier when they became trapped between rock groups.

In some places several young landed close to each other. These rose and instinctively banded together for company and their massed piping was loud. Some became wedged between jagged stones that made walking along the edge of the low tide a dangerous and slow process. One after another we found them, gathered them in batches and placed them in the sea. They were immensely strong for their size, and struggled wildly, pecking at our fingers with hard stabs of the dark beaks.

Reaching the very edge of the small waves, they would wait for a moment, listening for the growling voice of their own parent. From all the mass of shouting out in the bay each of these hordes of eager young had to find the old bird that would accept it. In some remarkable manner the young knew its parent's growl and the adult its youngster's high piping, and pair after pair met some way out from the shore.

It was an amazing performance to watch. It was also filled with danger for the young, and though we managed to avert it in some measure that danger is a part of the life and death drama of the cliffs each season.

Those who survived the falls and began their walking and running to the shore faced the black-backed gulls. These vicious killers had waited with a grim patience and had gathered in strength. The ravens had also come from long distances along the cliffs, but our presence kept them at a respectful distance and they voiced their anger in long clanging 'korp, korp' calls that echoed from the cliff face.

Gull after gull swooped to pluck up a struggling piping guillemot or razorbill from the grass or from between the rocks.

A vicious nip from the big yellow beaks of the black-backs and the shrill calls ceased and the small bodies hung limp and lifeless as they were carried back to low stones by the water. With several gulps the killers swallowed their victims and were ready to hunt again.

We were powerless to prevent many of the youngsters meeting such a fate so quickly after their fall from the cliffs, but if we had not been there night after night then the slaughter would have been far greater, for the ravens would have added their beaks to the already formidable array of death-dealing bills waiting to hack the black and white young to pieces.

Many of the small swimming birds were also taken by the gulls as they sped over the water with all the speed they could manage. This infuriated us, for there seemed no reason whatever why the parents should not have swum quickly towards their young and given them their protection. They made no move to do so, however, being content to remain some considerable distance out in the bay, calling the whole time. Their apparent stupidity annoyed us even more than the attacks of the gulls. A slight effort on the part of the adult razorbills and guillemots and a great many youngsters could have been saved every night.

Farther along where the sheep path began to rise upwards along the cliff face and the sea was directly underneath, conditions were much better. There the parent, or in some cases both parents, flew from the ledges and holes above us when we were high on the track, keeping close to the side of the struggling young. The pair or the three birds would all descend to the water together, hitting the surface with a loud plop. They would then immediately begin to swim away into the deep water until they were far from the nesting cliffs.

The experience of standing under these ledges while pair after pair fly directly over one's head down to the water is fascinating. The wings move with a whirring speed, and one watches the struggling dropping flight of the small birds with the fervent hope that they will reach the water and not hit the rocks directly under them. Their launching flight takes them some distance away from the cliff face, however, so usually all is well.

The black-backed gulls were certainly the most persistent and never-absent killers among the rocks and the cliffs at Vaeroy. The whole time we were on the islands they were never far from the nesting colonies of terns, gulls, eiders, oystercatchers, guillemots, razorbills, kittiwakes or even ringed plovers. No bird would leave its eggs for any length of time without the risk of them being taken by black-backed gulls or even by ravens. The ravens were also feared and hated foes, ranging on their black wings along the whole lengths of cliffs and shore rocks.

But it was the black-backed gulls who were always there, even on the watch. Standing very often in pairs, their beady dark eyes missed very little of what happened around them. They had their own eggs and young on isolated small isles where they seemed to have good success with their hatchings. But their patrols were made all day over the incubating birds or along the ledges of the cliffs.

The guillemot and razorbill young, who survived the ordeal of the rocks and grass between the cliff and the sea and eventually met up with their parents on the water, had begun a journey that would keep them on the open waves for long months. During these autumn swims into the depths of the ocean wastes, their flight feathers would grow, and the old birds would be able to moult and shed their faded summer feathering.

The razorbills did not nest in such large colonies as the guillemots. They preferred to be in small groups or even single scattered pairs, and although they could have their attractive large single eggs on ledges, as the guillemots did, there was a greater tendency to hide the egg under rocks or in the cracks of the cliffs.

Both the immaculate black and white parent razorbills had taken their share of the hours spent incubating the egg, and from their ledges and holes had been heard a continuous low purring growl that seemed more musical than the harsh 'ooorrrr, oorrrr' cries of the guillemots. The razorbills always seemed to be under some stress when they were incubating. They could not sit or remain still over the egg for any length of time, and at the slightest alarm they were ready to take wing. Those that showed the greatest calmness were the non-nesting immature birds who gathered in large preening groups close to the water.

For generations the fishermen and their sons have clambered along the ledges of the cliff face, or been lowered at the end of double ropes early each summer after the laying of the first batch of eggs. To the families who live close to the wildness of the sea, the birds and their eggs have always provided a welcome and valuable extra food supply. Salted and preserved, both bird and egg have added variety to the diet that could grow very monotonous. From the sea an endless supply of rich protein and vitamins has been taken throughout the year. Fish have never deserted the waters around the Lofotens. They, together with the countless millions of sea birds, have returned with the spring light, or even in the winter gloom, for centuries.

Lower down on the immense slopes, thickly covered with cracks, small caves and grottoes, and narrow ledges, the kittiwakes return to claim their nesting ledges long before their eggs are laid. Their wailing rang in our ears, mingling with the crashing of the breakers on the shore rocks under them, for the whole of the summer.

Between the lowest jumbles of boulders over which the storms so often flung sheets of white spray, the black guillemots nested in loose colonies: friendly little auks in black coats with vivid white wing patches.

Among the driftwood, wherever we tramped, pair after pair of oystercatchers had their living space. As soon as we left the territory of one pair, others would take up the penetrating, far-reaching 'kleeping' alarm calls. Here on the island they seemed to belong. Their cries mingled with the long musical trills of the curlew pairs nesting on the sides of the slopes, the sharper strident shouts of the whimbrels or the lonely wild notes of the redshanks. The whole blended to form a concerto of the sea with the crashing of the waves as a fitting accompaniment . . .

Over all these various birds, with their carefully concealed eggs and camouflaged hidden young, constantly winged their foes . . . greater black-backed gulls and their companions the herring gulls, Arctic skuas, the deep croaking ravens, and above them all, the majestic sea eagles.

Perhaps those that had had least to fear from these foes all summer had been the delightful snow buntings, the colourful and very welcome wheatears, the charming and fearless wagtails, and the host of sober-hued pipits, all of whom had laid their eggs under stones or in holes in the sides of grassy banks.

They had brought splashes of welcome extra colouring to a world that was dominated by black and white. The cliff faces had a speckled appearance as the masses of puffins, razorbills and guillemots covered them with their neat white and black coats. The delicate terns and gulls, too, were white and black, as was the greater black-backed gull, while the raven was attired in a feathering suitable for an undertaker.

Only the lonely soaring sea eagles sailing over the cliffs day after day, summer and winter, had plumage that merged so well into the mottled background of the rocks as to make them almost invisible on their summits. When they alighted on a favourite ledge their brown feathers blended into the patterns made by the grey and black lichens and the general colouring of the cliff face, and they seemed to disappear. But they also missed very little of what happened in the restless world over which they silently winged.

The flickering yellow flame of the candle, never still in the draught, made the spidery handwriting covering the pages of my diary dance and seem to assume life. Turning back through the pages, my mind was again filled with the dramas and adventures of the past few months. Living and sleeping close to the millions of wings flying without pause and with so little rest in the eternal light of a sun that never drops below the horizon for the weeks of high summer—this indeed had been an experience that could not be forgotten.

The days of early May again came vividly to my mind . . . the massed risings of thousands of kittiwakes from their preening rocks by the edge of the restless waves, each bird responding as if to a word of command . . . the first sight of the sea eagles patrolling along the sheer high face of the great cliffs . . . the huge almost silent flotillas of puffins, guillemots and razorbills facing into the wind and riding the waves for hours at a time in the bay . . . the first blooms of the northern wild flowers that were later to make such a remarkable sight of floral beauty among the rocks of the islands . . . the unforgettable thrill of watching the sea eagle return-ing with fish to her eyrie high on the cliffs in the light of the early dawn sky . . . the massed guillemots springing from the rough swell at the base of the rocks in the jumping manner of penguins . . . the world of the newly arrived gannets . . . the force and power of the sea to which we were so closely bound . . .

These impressions, and so many others, had been written each evening after our meal round a driftwood fire in the open between the rocks, or in the small room at the old wooden school-house.

The nature world of North Norway has a strange and powerful lure that becomes stronger year by year as the domain over which the eagles fly shrinks more and more. The high lonely peaks around

B

the Lofoten chain, and the isolated bird rocks that rear out of the
sea in great grey heights around Röst and Vaeroy, remain strongholds for the sea birds and the sea eagles in a world where freedom
to live an undisturbed life in conditions unpolluted by man grows
ever more difficult.

The storm slowly abates, leaving our world damp and cold in the
wake of the winds. On the slopes the thick vegetation that rises high
on the sides of the cliffs is enriched with a welcome harvest of delicious blueberries and the big golden cloudberries.

Over the slopes the willow grouse whirr on fast-beating white
wings. 'Go-beck, go-beck'. . . the old birds warn us constantly,
when we come too close to their large families of rapidly growing
young, hiding between the rocks by the sides of the streams filled
with rain water.

The eagles swoop down and pluck an occasional young grouse
from its hiding place. It gives variety to their diet. As a family the
eagles soar high above us . . . here they have been able to rear
their young for another year.

The thick fogs return to swirl around the tops of the mountains
. . . It is nearly time to leave.

2 *Return of the Birds*

Into the North Atlantic like a long crooked finger juts the forbidding yet remarkably varied and rich range of islands known as the Lofoten Wall. In places the islands have an alpine scenery, mountain peaks being crested with snow patches even in midsummer. The chain reaches out from the mainland over a wide sound known as the Vestfjord. Crossing the great water in very early summer, with the thick fogs covering the tops of the grey mountains and the air cold and harsh to the face, it is possible to appreciate a little of the grimness of winter in this region above the Arctic Circle.

A thousand years ago the Vikings explored northwards in their open longships, landing on the Lofotens and discovering the value of cod dried on lines to the hardness of tough wood. In January the deep-swimming cod come down from the cold Barents Sea to spawn in the waters around the Lofotens, warmed by the Gulf Stream. Throughout the centuries these waters have drawn armies of fishermen to the huge spawning grounds.

From the fishing villages along the mainland came fleets of

open boats, with central masts and big square brown sails, rowed by several pairs of strong arms. For several months they would have to brave the storms of the Vestfjord and, in a similar manner to their ancestors the Vikings, they prayed to their God for safety before setting out. Some were destined never to return, for the seas of winter claimed many victims.

When the storms proved too fierce even for the hardy men of North Norway, then the boats had to be beached on some lonely island. Lying on the rocks with keel upwards, they were used as rough shelters in the darkness and biting winds.

The whole saga of the Lofotens has been written round the migrating cod; the tough, hard-drinking men who fought nature and each other to drag their share of the harvest from the seas from January until the end of March, and the teeming millions of sea birds who faithfully returned to the cliffs in the wake of the retreating cod.

The open boats and the harsh winter expeditions are no more. The boats have been replaced by fast, strong motor vessels with equipment for detecting the shoals of fish in the deep water of the open sea. Each season, fewer men take quantities of fish that would have been the envy of the older fishermen with their more primitive equipment. The standard of living is now high. No longer do the men and the boys have to swing down the sides of the great cliffs to gather eggs in their thousands.

Millions of dried cod still hang in the wind on long lines over every Lofoten village by the sea, drying to a hard toughness until June. The smell of the fish casts a heavy unshakeable odour, despite the winds, over the villages.

Snow falls in the dark autumn days when the sun is never to be seen: a snow covering the mountains and the cliffs that are silent where all was noise and life in summer.

The gloom is defeated by the gleam of the sun returning in January, when it again glows as a deep orange ball low over the horizon for a short time. It gains in strength, rising higher each day.

The men of the fishing villages have sweated with the strain of the months when they must bring back their boats loaded with the heavy cod that filled the waters close to the Lofoten islands. Later in the year they will be able to relax for then the fish will have departed until the next January.

Towards the end of February the birds return. First come the black guillemots, the early spring cold light shining on their bright white wing patches and the brilliant coral-red feet spread out high behind them as they fly in low and fast over the waves.

With the arrival of March the kittiwakes begin to assemble in big flocks, returning from their scattered winter flights over vast areas of the oceans. It is then too early to think of nesting, but they endlessly weave in restless flight around the ledges they will eventually use for their eggs.

Later in the month the trills of the oystercatchers are heard all around the islands. They bring back a splash of bold black and white and orange to the grey landscape. Also in March the massed armies of the guillemots and the razorbills appear, swimming in huge flotillas in the seas around their nesting cliffs.

They are followed by the puffins, winging back in their millions from an unknown winter habitat. The lonely vastness of the open seas have given them food, and their small black and white bodies have thick, tight feathering that keeps them buoyant and warm in the swells far from land. They remain swimming around the cliffs, not approaching the high slopes in which they have their long tunnels until well into April.

With the warmer days of early May, the Arctic skuas appear suddenly in the night. They also have roamed far from land all winter. Now they return for their season as pirates of the air.

In June, when the air is further warmed, the delicate Arctic terns are again screeching over their nesting rocks close to the edge of the water. They have probably completed a longer winter journey than any of the other birds of the lonely islands.

Around the fishing villages the eiders have swum in solemn groups all winter. But the giant massed flocks have been far out at sea. Many favour the ice-free waters off south-western Greenland, where both they and the colourful king eiders have been killed in enormous numbers every winter for centuries.

In the far north areas of the wintering regions are to be found mostly the young birds hatched in the previous summer. These immature birds haunt the rocks close to the shore, feeding mainly on snails and bivalves on the shallow sea bottom.

The handsome male eiders are elegant in their black and white, with pale green patches behind the head and a rosy hue to their white breasts. They have lain in big flocks off-shore in the north in early spring. From far over the water I have listened to the wild music of their calls . . . 'aahhooo-aahhooo' . . . as they swim in big flocks. The sober dull brownish ducks encourage them with low growling answers which seem to excite the drakes.

The slaughter of eiders in winter has always been immense. In southern Greenland a valuable extra income has been earned for many years by making blankets and wall-carpets from the skins of these birds. As up to a hundred skins, from which the soft down has not been removed, are needed for such a carpet, even for this purpose the killing has been great. The blanket is finished with a decorative edging of feathers from the handsome drakes and also the ducks, and there has always been a ready sale for such examples of skilled craft work.

For generations the soft and warm down from the breasts of the ducks has been taken from the nests for filling eiderdowns and other items needing very light and warm padding. But the birds no longer return to their nesting islands in such huge numbers as in former years. Constant disturbance of their colonies has forced them to nest on islands where they have greater freedom and peace.

They have a fondness for the nearness of humans, however. Probably they feel a greater sense of safety from their many winged foes when they are close to the fishing sheds and the activity of the fishing villages. The villagers know this and prepare for the birds by arranging stones in groups, surmounted by slabs of rock under which the sitting birds can have protection from attack from above.

When the mated pairs feel the time has come to look for a site for the eggs, they come ashore in the very early morning quietness and examine these prepared refuges most carefully. Pair after pair finally decide on one of the sites or a place between the rocks in the open, and the silent still forms of the ducks can begin their long incubating vigil without the support of their mates.

The day was indeed cold and grey when our heavily loaded car was lifted by crane on to the deck of the small motor vessel *Röst* which plies between the mainland, the Lofotens and the outlying islands of Vaeroy and Röst. It was early in May and we were first headed towards Röst, several hours steaming into the North Atlantic.

Röst lies flat and windswept, its highest point being only a few yards from high-water level. Of trees there are none, and rocks and stagnant-water pools litter the island that has known tough fishing families for centuries. Behind the white wooden church, around which the sheep roam, is a wide lonely expanse of marshland. This is a favourite haunt of Arctic skuas, redshanks, snow buntings, wheatears and pipits, Lapland buntings and red phalaropes, preening kittiwakes and a great many waders. It is seldom visited, but I have spent many hours facing the winds and cold amid its rich bird life.

Close to Röst itself are the great rocks rising straight from the sea that make the village so known. The three bird islands together give breeding room to several million birds each season.

Some two hours' steaming time from Röst is Vaeroy. From the sea it appeared to us cold and greyly remote. It rose in a series of big bulging mountain masses. The white church showed clearly against the gloom of the background mountains, over which the sea eagles have soared for generations. We landed at eleven on a night so cold that it was difficult to believe it was May. Thankfully we unloaded our equipment into the rorbu we were to use as a headquarters. One of the many hundreds built in former years around the fishing villages, it had once housed the crew from a fishing boat far from its home village for the whole of the Lofoten cod season.

Behind our rorbu, with its wood-burning black iron stove, hung long lines of cod-heads, dried to a dirty hardness. The stench from them filled the interior of the room and soon penetrated into all our clothing.

Vaeroy is an island of grey rock. Only some 10 per cent of its surface is a thin soil, which during the years has been covered with a matted vegetation consisting of coarse grasses, heather, spongy mosses of many varieties, the strong binding stalks of crow and blueberries, and a mass of the glowing wild plants of the north. A tree is a rare sight, although some of the villagers have surrounded their houses with mountain ash and willow which withstand the winter winds very well.

Sheep have roamed the windswept slopes for generations, making narrow paths all over the mountain sides right to the summits. Housed in sheds all winter when snow covers the slopes, and fed mainly on the hay so carefully scythed from between the rocks in July, they wander freely over the island from early spring until late autumn.

On the farther arm of the great bay over the water from the village of Vaeroy, we could glimpse Mostad. The village faced the sea, meeting the force of the winds as they whined to the shore. But the folds of the precipitous cliffs that gave summer nesting room to the millions of auks and kittiwakes also gave it a measure of protection from the worst of the weather.

High above the almost overhanging range behind the village, sea eagles had their lonely isolated eyries, far from the paths of man. The village was not entirely devoid of human life. Monrad Mickelssen, 'the last of the Vikings' as he is called in the Lofoten range, remained, with his wife, as a lonely guardian of the rocks and the birds.

In a small fishing boat whose engine coughed and spluttered, we crossed the bay on a clear but cold May morning. The morning sun illuminated with its yellow glow the towering cliff range behind Mostad. The houses strung along the waterfront were sharply etched against the deep grey and dark green of the rocks. Their woodwork had not known fresh paint for many years: the white and red of the houses was faded and forlorn.

Rounding the jutting cliff forming one arm of the small natural shallow harbour along which the village had been built, we were immediately plunged into choppy steel-grey seas, with a biting wind that stung our eyes. Groups of black shags flew in alarm as our swaying noisy boat came close to their perching-rocks.

The waves eased slightly as we neared the cliffs rising directly from the deep water. There are no natural landing places here at all. Around us floated massed armies of guillemots, puffins and razorbills. The sight was indeed impressive on such a day.

These northern razorbills were very striking with their strong wide flattened beaks. Big flocks would now also be gathering around the coast of West Greenland, eastern Canada and even farther eastwards. During the winter they had spread over a wide area from southern Norway to Portugal, with huge flocks in the Danish waters.

Those that found their nesting sites around the coasts of Britain, in Icelandic waters and around the Faeroe Islands and Heligoland have a somewhat shorter beak, with smaller wings. Those that favoured the Scottish coastal islands and mainland also mostly wintered in western Scandinavia.

All these sea birds had been drawn back in the early cold months of spring to the waters around their nesting cliffs. The urge to examine the ledges and rocks was still weak, however. Days and nights had been spent in great flocks swimming and diving and performing massed formation movements as if under a single command. One moment the sea could be covered with their black forms and the next be empty as they dived in unison.

Later in April they had suddenly left the sea and winged back to study their nesting ledges for a while. The razorbills had then shown a greater desire to separate into small groups or even single pairs. But the guillemots kept in their big groups, the immature young, who would not yet nest, keeping to the lower shore rocks.

On this cold and blustery day in May with the choppy sea slapping against the sides of our small craft, time was still passing in idle play and mating between the pairs on the water.

At the approach of our boat with its unwelcome noisy engine, the great floating army of birds became obsessed with the urgent desire to put as much space between them and us as quickly as possible. Many dived, whilst others tried to take to the air.

Showers of water from the threshing of thousands of webbed feet shot into the air as the birds tried to gain momentum to rise. Wings flapped madly, but it was not easy for the birds to fly from the waves. Group by group they eventually rose, flying very low into the distance away from us. A few razorbills swung round and round over us on strong plump bodies, wings beating very fast. They were obviously more curious than alarmed.

Mixed in with the flocks of guillemots and razorbills were the other delightful little auks, the puffins. They pulled crimson webbed feet as high as possible behind them as they flapped on fast, whirring small wings over the waves and away from the boat. Many dived to reappear and stare at us curiously. Shags also appeared, pushing up long thin necks above the surface in the manner of periscopes.

From all these many thousands of birds, filling the air with the swish of their black wings, there came no other sound. There were no alarm cries whatever. These were to come from the restless kittiwakes, with a wailing volume of sound that grew so loud that we could not converse.

As we neared the cliffs the kittiwakes voiced their interest in our boat by a renewed and heightened chorus of 'kit-eee-wake' cries that swelled into a mighty roar of sound as the huge silent wide-winged form of a patrolling sea eagle swept along the upper face of their nesting cliff.

Every bird rose to the attack, wailing in an almost pathetic shrill manner as they attacked their foe from all sides. Twisting and turning in its efforts to escape their flashing wings, the eagle rose and gave a high sharp yelp of annoyance and frustration. It was as yet too early for the kittiwakes to have eggs in their deep cup nests of dried weeds, glued to the narrow rock ledges. But later in the season the eagles would have good hunting among these many thousands of restive birds.

The eagles themselves already had eggs over which the female had patiently sat for many days. Their windswept eyrie high among the mountain peaks had been carefully selected for its remoteness from their only real foe, man.

Deep croaking clanking calls of 'korp, korp, korp' from ravens added to the general uproar along the rocky and broken face of the cliff. The earliest of all the northern birds to lay their eggs in the dark cracks high up on one of the more remote cliff sides, the ravens would also patrol these nesting sites all summer, picking off young birds and adults until the last of the hordes departed in autumn.

The sea eagles and the ravens were the rulers of these cliffs. In their strong beaks and claws they had the power of life and death. They were feared and hated by the millions of winged inhabitants of all the ledges and holes.

Between these killers there was no feeling but dislike, and the aerial contests between the yelping eagles and the croaking ravens were thrilling displays we were to witness many times in June.

Life along these cliffs was hard. Each species kept closely to its own kind, ignoring its neighbours. Where the species mingled and overlapped, as when the kittiwakes and guillemots shared the same ledges, although there was irritation between the birds, fighting only occurred between those of the same species.

Nature has arranged a set of rules that all had to obey. Whilst the rules were followed, then the balance of the cliff-face populations would be observed. The grim slaughter from the many foes of the massed sea birds was all part of an ordered plan.

As the boat tossed and came dangerously close to the jutting rocks with their showers of white spray being flung back to us, I pondered upon the reason why these northern waters have some of the greatest gatherings of sea birds in the world all summer.

Just as the seas around the Lofotens, containing a vast quantity of plankton and small fish, provide food for the spawning, deep-swimming cod each season, so they provide a rich spring and summer diet for the birds that return year by year to the same rocks from which they were hatched.

In the higher Arctic seas the appearance each spring of the microscopic algae holds the secret of the abundance of life on which both fish and birds find the means of survival in such vast numbers.

The development of these algae is perhaps the most important phenomenon of the Arctic year, affecting all life in the seas much farther south. These phytoplankton form the basis for all animal life in the oceans, being the only food for the small planktonic crustaceans known as krill on which the fish and many species of sea birds feed.

In winter and very early spring the light in the Arctic regions is much too weak to be used by the plants for an effective assimilation of the carbon dioxide they need, even in the upper water layers.

The phytoplankton are therefore only represented by spores all winter. During this long dark period when nearly all life has departed from the far north, nutritive salts in the form of nitrates and phosphates accumulate in large amounts. They are utilised by the plants on the return of the light in early spring.

When the sun again mounts steadily higher, regaining its power in May in the high Arctic, then an explosion of phytoplankton production occurs. Almost simultaneously the crustaceans develop in huge numbers, feeding on the algae with which the seas so suddenly swarm.

This remarkable growth of the phytoplankton production in the Arctic seas is of very short duration, usually lasting about a month, after which the nutritive salts are exhausted. In the regions where the upsurge of cold bottom water supplies the upper layers with new quantities of nutritive material, however, the production of this invaluable phytoplankton can continue for up to a further two months. These upsurges of cold water occur at the meeting places of the currents of the oceans, at the borders of glaciers and icebergs, and other such suitable places.

The life of the great plankton masses is short. By high summer the phytoplankton has disappeared, not to reappear until the cycle commences again in the following year with the return of the light.

The nesting sea birds must desert the Arctic seas for the greater part of the year. Scattering widely over the oceans in search of the food that has been so plentiful all summer, they return to their home nesting cliffs as soon as the urge to wing back becomes strong.

In the high Arctic regions in very unfavourable years a large number of the birds have already left again in July. Then there is no nesting and the birds keep together in big restless flocks until they again depart in the lonely wastes of the oceans.

But such non-breeding years are unknown among the birds around Röst and Vaeroy where the waters, warmed by the Gulf Stream, are extremely rich in food. In certain years that are unfavourable there *can* be difficulty in obtaining enough to feed many millions. The puffins, guillemots and razorbills, needing great quantities of fish, lay only one egg for each breeding pair, probably for this reason, but the black guillemots try to rear two youngsters if possible. Kittiwakes, feeding on the surface krill, find their food much more easily than the auks, and can usually manage to rear two very attractive young on their massed nesting ledges.

If the early eggs are taken, as they have been for generations in such huge numbers, then the birds will lay again after several days. If no further eggs are taken, then the numbers will be maintained, but if the ledges and holes are plundered several times then it is not possible for the birds to have a successful breeding that season.

Stoats, wild mink and sea-otters are foes with which the black guillemots have to fight, as well as the waves dashing into their holes. They are fortunate if they manage to rear the youngsters that are fully feathered and ready to fly when they eventually face the world some forty days after being hatched.

It is along these northern Norwegian coasts and islands that the auks and other sea birds attain such immense numbers all summer. It is one of the reasons why the sea eagles have also always been plentiful, and why Vaeroy has been one of their main strongholds through the centuries.

The towering cliffs rose almost straight above us, pale grey blotched with green in the light of the sun. A jump from the boat to the rocks jutting like teeth out of the water at their base seemed impossible in such weather. Our tough Norwegian helper, Ronald Johanssen, was not to be daunted, however. Taking a great risk and scraping his boat against the shore rocks, he held it steady with muscles that swelled with the strain, whilst we sprang at the exact second on to a narrow ledge. We sprawled on its wet surface for a moment to recover our balance.

Kittiwakes almost brushed our faces with their wing tips. Below us the water gleamed with an almost unnatural green. Slowly and carefully we climbed upwards and soon could look down into the still empty nests of the kittiwakes. Shags balanced on rocks in the strong wind, top crests blowing forward.

Farther above us, where the loose rocks had piled through the centuries as they dropped from the tops of the peaks, an illegal trapper of puffins had set up a long net over some of the nesting holes. Some 15 yards long by some 2 yards deep, the net had already caught and killed several of the birds. As we looked up at it, another bird was trapped as it flew into the mesh, and began to struggle furiously.

Ulla-Maija, whose exploits in former years in the high mountain farther north had earned her the respect of the tough fishermen, showed her anger by a string of Finnish oaths. Scrambling upwards on the slippery scree, she reached the net and tore at the mesh, breaking it in several places. She released the bird still living and slid downwards again to the ledge on which I was crouched. Ronald Johanssen had to remain in control of the boat to prevent it being smashed against the cliffs.

The little bird with the ruby-red eyes and grotesque highly coloured flattened beak regarded us quietly with an unblinking stare. The white feathering of its breast was very thick and close, ideal for its watery life all winter. The bird shook itself and then flew with narrow whirring wings down to the sea, its feet making a splash of crimson as the sun caught them.

The wind rose higher to a piercing shriek and it was impossible to stay longer on these exposed ledges on such a day. Ronald Johanssen had perhaps been rather reckless in landing us, but he showed considerable courage and strength in again getting the boat into a position where we could almost throw ourselves into its tossing space.

Soon we were soaked by the spray into which the bows plunged deeply, and the surplus water had to be baled from the bottom of the boat. Mostad and its cliffs receded in size as we struggled over the bay that was now much too stormy for such a small boat.

Thankful to be back on the dry rocks, we needed the heat from our driftwood fire to dry out our clothing and give us welcome warmth.

In our rorbu, the rain had begun to beat against the window-panes facing the sea. The cold rawness made us aware that whatever date the calendar might say, here the forces of nature were the rulers. Humans who invaded these territories had to accept the constant changes of weather, following the winds and rains with periods of sun and calm. No two days or nights seemed to be alike, but all too often the whine of the wind was to greet us as we rose from our sleeping-bags in the early mornings.

3 Life among the Living Rocks

In early May there is a general air of greyness over the island of Vaeroy. Even the grass, now freed from its covering of snow, is still bleakly and coldly grey-green.

The windswept rocks are enlivened by the first of the colourful and impressive displays of wild plants of the northern world. As we trek in the gloom of the overhanging clouds caressing the tops of the cliffs above us, the heroic little purple saxifrage glows with patches of pale brightness among the rocks. The flowers are indeed welcome.

Even in the high Arctic this little plant is the first to show its purple blooms as soon as the snow recedes. These early specimens have no long stalks: to lessen exposure to the desiccating winds they are cushioned on thick spongy moss-like bases that fasten firmly to the rocks or earth.

Many of the snow-bed plants of the far north benefit from the protection against the cold winds that the snow offers for several months. Under a thick and warming layer of white they can develop, ready to burst into full bloom as soon as they are released to the light. There is no long spring as we know it in England. With the rise in temperature, the disappearance of the snow, and

Page 33 (above) Young guillemots, survivors of the drop from their high cliff ledges, listen to the calls of their parents out at sea before scurrying to the water; (below) razorbill young in early August

Page 34 (*above*) Released from an illegal trapping net, the puffin escapes to the sea; (*below*) kittiwakes perched on shore rocks waiting to begin nesting on ledges along the cliffs

the daylight that never fades for many weeks in summer, all vegetation grows at a truly remarkable rate.

The little saxifrage was the first to appear on the northern face of the island, where the winds blow in unchecked fury direct from the sea. Here the precipitous cliffs receive its full force as they rise cold and grey from the edge of the water. A little above the huge breakers that roll in to pound with sullen anger against their base, thousands of kittiwakes have their nesting ledges, and above them the auks.

On a low plateau of short grass at the base of the cliffs where the boulders lie in scattered confusion, a pool of fresh water has been formed by an underground spring. Here the kittiwakes gather in big bathing parties. Throughout the day the water is filled with a mass of white birds, splashing their wings with a great flurry that can be heard some distance away. Kittiwakes spend much time at their toilet, dipping heads under water and shaking wings with much energy until they feel they can fly off to the big dark preening boulders at the edge of the sea. There they sit for hours, carefully preening their feathering until it is immaculate. Around the edge of the pool lies a thick white layer of discarded feathers, and as one party of birds leaves the bathing place another flies in from along the cliff face to land with much commotion.

The only time I have known the kittiwakes to be silent is when they sit in great masses, covering the preening rocks as if with a layer of snow. Facing into the cold wind, they remain silent for a long period until as though from a sudden command they rise as one bird, exploding with whiteness into the air.

Swinging round in a short flight they return to settle again. They are restless and anxious to start their egg laying, but the days are still bitterly cold and they wait for warmer weather.

Around the pool lines of sheep, with many new-born lambs, pass on their way to the heights.

The lonely flat landscape of ragged rocks pushing out like a long finger to form the southern arm of the big bay at Vaeroy is the summer haunt of many birds: common gulls, eiders, Arctic

c

skuas, ringed plovers, oystercatchers, many wheatears, and a shower of bright meadow pipits. Many waders spend hours poking amid the very thick fringe of strong deep brown seaweeds, and lapwings tumble over them at times, seeming out of place in this world.

Over them all the bully of the rocks, the greater black-backed gull, maintains a constant watch. But even this feared predator falls victim to the claws and beak of the sea eagles, for whom these rocks are a hunting ground for much of their summer food.

The common gulls have not yet begun to lay, although they rise in a noisy wheeling group when we approach their rocks, dashing down close to our heads in their anger. They are usually destined to lose their first clutch of eggs, for the villagers and the black-backs seem to take them all. Only when they lay again do they appear to have better luck, but the number of young who eventually fly from the island in autumn is never large.

In one of the many small sheltered spots between the rocks by the tide edge, six pairs of eiders feed. The weeds are rich with insects and small crustaceans, and into this thick bed of rubbery weed in the shallow water the eiders constantly up-end. The common gulls also pick with great daintiness at the menu provided by the weeds, as do the oystercatchers, who poke about with their long probing orange beaks for hour after hour as the tide recedes.

At frequent intervals the ducks of the eiders encourage mating on the quiet water. They appear at this stage of their mating always to be the partner making the first move. Stretching their heads and necks along the surface of the green water, they remain close beside their handsome males.

At first the drakes ignore these invitations, but the ducks persist, and suddenly without warning there is a flurry of water as one after another the drakes spring upon the backs of the ducks, grab a beakful of neck feathers as though in a burst of temper, and perform the mating act in a matter of seconds. The ducks immediately begin a careful washing and flapping of the wings which seems to give them a good deal of satisfaction. Probably they feel instinctively they must encourage all the mating they can at this time of calm before the serious summer breeding. Very soon now they will be left alone, widows of the rocks for the summer.

Very early in spring long strings of eiders begin their migration northwards again, heading up as far as the high Arctic waters, where they mingle with large gatherings of auks. At their resting places at the heads of some of the deep fjords of North Norway I have watched their mating ceremonies, which are somewhat different to their performances on the Vaeroy water in the early days of May! The males in the glory of their breeding plumage pursue the ducks with a persistence that is often resented. Jerking their beaks back until they point to the sky, the drakes utter their attractive calls of the spring . . . 'aahh-oo, aahh-oo'. From the groups of ducks come the answering low notes . . . 'orr-orr-orr'.

The days of April, when the snow still lies over the fjord slopes and the sun can glitter with a blinding brilliance on the calm water, are also musically enriched with the lovely calls of the long-tailed ducks. From far out in the deep water of the fjords the sound has reached me when I was surrounded by several hundred reindeer waiting to cross the fjord at the end of their spring migration trek . . . 'Aahlu-et-aah' . . . it is certainly one of the most fascinating and appealing sounds of the early spring that I have heard in the north.

The mating displays of these charming ducks are delightful to witness. The males swim around their selected mates, long tail feathers erect, neck extended and beak pointing skyward. The long musically echoing calls are repeated time after time until the females respond.

Both eiders and long-tailed ducks choose their mates on the waters of their winter quarters. From that time onwards the drakes remain faithfully and constantly at their side. Each time the duck flies a short distance over the sea or fjord surface the drake will immediately follow her. There seems to me no marriage so close at this period, and none so broken by distance later in the summer, as that of the eiders.

Until the day the eggs are laid the drake remains a very attentive mate. The ducks are very fat at this time, as they need to be, for a long period of fasting lies ahead. On Vaeroy we watched several pairs carefully investigating possible sites between the rocks until they found spots that pleased them. The ducks appeared so heavy that they could hardly waddle over the stones, but the drakes escorted them the whole while as though they were real beauties of the bird world.

Among the colony of common gulls was the favourite place for most of the down-lined nests when the ducks eventually felt the time had come in May to nest. But one pair we followed decided they liked the isolation of the cliff side, where it sloped up from the sea, covered with springy vegetation. On the top of a projecting rock from which the duck had a clear view over the water quite a long distance below, the nest was made and well hidden. When the duck had laid her four large pale greenish eggs she made a last visit to the sea to feed and drink. Then she returned and when she had settled over the eggs her colouring blended so well into the undergrowth as to make her almost invisible.

Her long melancholy face watched impassively as the drake swam for hours at a time in the quiet bay below the cliff. He seemed at a loss to know how to pass the time, and eventually he and other drakes began to gather in a large group.

For three weeks the duck would have to cover the incubating eggs, never leaving them during the day. Only late at night, when the predators had ceased their patrolling for a short while, would she leave the nest to fly down to the water for a quick bathe and drink. She would eat nothing, and the fat with which she had commenced the incubation period would sustain her until the eggs hatched.

Other ducks had selected sites completely in the open between rocks or even among the driftwood. They were as still and silent as the rocks and wood around them, and almost impossible to detect. Their absolute stillness served as camouflage and protection against the sea eagles and other foes.

The drakes had remained for a few days, some of them flirting with the immature ducks who had no eggs but were present in large numbers all summer at the nesting rocks. But the drakes soon seemed to tire of this and one morning they left in a big flotilla, to be seen no more. To the uninitiated it seems a strange way to behave, but there is a good reason for their actions.

The drakes would move along the coast for some time, joining forces with one-year-old immature birds until they began their moult in the middle of July. This was the time of their shame and they remained far out to sea if possible. Their immaculate black and white feathering was replaced by a mottled and untidy plumage resembling to a certain extent that of the females. This eclipse dress period found them almost helpless and needing the protection of dull feathering. The flight feathers had to be renewed, and the eiders would be unable to fly at all until they were. In the duck and geese families, as well as the divers and auks, the quills are shed simultaneously, and in the flightless weeks that follow the birds are very vulnerable to attacks from the air.

The drakes were much better far out of the way, for when the eggs on which the ducks were sitting broke and the young emerged, they would dry in a few hours and the fluffy chicks would be ready to tumble into the water in the wake of the parent.

The nest we had discovered high on the side of the slopes above the low rocks remained unmolested by winged foes or by humans, who took most of the first eggs of the ducks nesting among the common gulls. As the days of May passed and the many grasses and flowers began to show in an ever greater profusion of gay colours, we waited for the morning to arrive when the duck would take her brood the long way down the cliff side to the sea.

Where the winds blew unchecked, hitting the sheer cliff sides with a moaning bitterness, the toughest of all the northern birds had found an ideal site for an early nest of thick twigs liberally and deeply lined with sheep wool. A raven pair, ruling over a very large territory, as each pair did at Vaeroy, already had young in a nest well hidden close to the top of the cliff and in a deep ledge into which the sun never shone.

Completely at home in conditions varying from the heat of the Sahara desert to the bitter coldness of the high Arctic winters, the ravens nest earlier than all other birds, even in the Arctic. Their eggs had been laid long before any of the sea birds now gathered around the cliffs would have felt any desire to incubate. During the bad early weather the female raven had not left the nest at all, for the eggs needed all her body warmth day and night. She was fed during this time by the black-coated male. We watched him searching at all hours of the day and long into the light evenings for anything edible among the rocks. When he flew back to the nest his harsh croaking calls echoed all along the cliff face, and whenever another raven came too close to his territory he immediately went to the attack.

Ravens have no real enemies apart from man, but the many youngsters who patrol with their parents along the mountainsides later in the summer meet their death by one means or another in winter, and the population seems to remain fairly constant. The old birds mostly prefer to stay close to their territory throughout the year, although some band together in dark flocks and fly southwards.

They are bitterly disliked by the oystercatchers, who have also divided up the shoreline into a series of territories which each pair jealously guards against all comers, whether they are ravens, Arctic skuas or black-backs and herring gulls.

In these early May days the oystercatchers run in pairs close to the edge of the tide. They keep close together and if one flies off for a short distance to forage among the seaweed, then its mate will quickly follow. A passing raven is greeted with a storm of abuse and a rise to attack by the flashing showy pairs. As yet they have no nests, but a strong instinct for controlling the air space over the spot where their eggs will be laid keeps them always on the alert.

The purple saxifrage has exhausted its brave showing, and has faded at the time when other early plants are opening. The grass is a warmer and deeper green, and each day more lambs appear. They take shelter from the winds between rocks upon which the sun strikes and which give them some warmth.

The great winter shoals of cod have disappeared into the deep oceans for another summer. The men can relax for the fishing has been good and their income high.

Golden plovers, handsome in their breeding plumage of black, white and golden brown, move over the short rain-soaked grass close to the shore rocks. They run forward, stop and listen and then probe into the soft earth for food. Several lapwings appear among them, and a pair of whimbrels stalk between the rocks, together with other waders. These are the early days when birds appear suddenly, remain for a short while and then are away. In the air is a feeling of spring restlessness and preparation for the summer breeding. Even an old grey heron with ragged wide wings has made its appearance, surprisingly far north for this bird. It stands for hours in the still water between the rocks, but takes flight when it sees us. Here it seems out of place and lonely.

Where the common gulls have now begun to lay their first attractive eggs in roughly made scrapes of grass between the sharp rocks close to the waves, the sea pinks have reddish heads as yet unopened. The delightful little *Silene acaulis* take over from the saxifrage in showing masses of small purple flowers on low cushions of green. There is sound and movement from the birds until late at night.

Many sober-hued but quietly attractive pipits, together with colourful wheatears, have already found sites between the stones and in grass banks. The wagtails are also back to brighten the rocks with their quick darting movements and bobbing tails. They find a rich supply of insects in their watery world by the shore line. As we move among the rocks they seem to find many insects that we have disturbed. They show no fear of us whatever.

Their fearlessness can be matched by that of the snow buntings, those delightful little snow-flakes of the north. Later we discovered a pair breeding alongside a pair of Arctic skuas, who had their eggs close to a very small pool on low swampy land. They ignored the dark-feathered predators completely as they built a nest of grasses between a pile of stones.

Later again, when they had young, we could sit within a few yards of them and watch both the very showy black and white male and the more quietly dressed female return time after time with beaks overflowing with insects. They found so many that some always fell to the rocks before the nest was reached. But they were always recovered. Overhead their piratical neighbours were chasing Arctic terns and kittiwakes in their harassing flight.

The wheatears had appeared in great numbers, showing their flashing white rumps between the rocks wherever we tramped under the sheer cliffs. Belonging to the Old World species, this hardy and charming little bird has invaded North America, from East Siberia to Alaska, and from Arctic Europe to Greenland and Baffin Bay. The birds we now saw in such numbers had no doubt wintered along the African coasts, and those that nested in Greenland and the eastern Arctic of Canada also travelled in autumn to these distant warm shores. Their migration routes entail long flights over the North Atlantic and the wheatear is the only passerine bird that faces such a broad ocean with its frequent September gales.

As the days of May passed and the weather became slowly warmer, so the thick heavy enveloping masses of cloud vapours gathered along the mountain tops. They shut out the sun, leaving us in gloom and dampness.

On the kittiwake ledges, that now resembled a giant beehive surrounded by never silent bees, nesting has begun. Even now it is early for them and there are few eggs. But the birds make a constant wailing chorus of protest when their ledges are approached. Deep grooves have been worn into the cliff face by the years of pounding seas. Over these, narrow ledges are filled with birds that are covered with spray in the summer storms. Not a single ledge can be found unoccupied, and mixing with them now are groups of razorbills, guillemots and puffins, standing on every available point of rock.

On their early morning patrols, in majestic flights that take them ever higher until they are lost to sight in the blue, the sea eagles watch over their domain. The ends of the long broad wings spread out like outstretched fingers. The wings move but rarely, for the air currents support the large birds as though they were weightless. With complete mastery of the air the eagles soar in wide circles over the cliffs, seeming to enjoy the effortless upward flights. No bird seems to use less energy in flight than the sea eagle, and even when it flies straight out to sea the wing movements are leisurely and relaxed.

With the first days of June the large orange ball of the sun remains above the horizon all night. Eternal daylight will mean that all growth will be rapid. There is little sound over the cliffs and rocks at midnight, and in the yellow glow over the water the outlying islands stand as dark silhouettes.

The warmth has encouraged the blooming of the flowers that make a wild garden of every possible crack on the cliffs. Where there appears to be no soil whatever the plants have managed to secure enough nourishment for their roots to hold them securely against the force of the fierce winds.

Shaking in every breeze the delicate little white *cerastium alpinum* clings to the cliff edges. The bold yellow flowers of the *caltha palustris* splash the low meadows around the houses with such an array of colour that they seem covered with a golden carpet. Purple *melandrium rubrum* add their quota of brightness to the grey cracks, whilst the lovely little star-shaped *trientalis europea* gleam like fallen stars against the darkness of the stones.

Yellow buttercups are now in full bloom, mixing with a great variety of long flowering grasses. And as the insects become more numerous they are attracted to the white heads of the *carum carvi*.

Where the sun strikes on the cliff face or between the sheltered rocks then it is indeed strong, and each day fresh flowers open to add their charm to this impressive collection for which the visitor is so unprepared. Nature compensates for the shortness of the summer by the intensity and vitality of the growth of all the vegetation.

After rain the jagged rocks that lie just above the high-water line, edged with their thick weed fringes, assume a wild artistic beauty. The bright heads of the sea pinks have now opened to gather in small clumps around the nests of the common gulls, and the rock itself is brightened to a remarkable contrasting colour scheme of orange, grey and black. The lichens, often taking the form of circles, blend and mingle to produce a harmonious set of patterns that are a never-ending delight. This art of nature has taken the weathering of countless years to perfect. Here there are colour schemes without faults as the very ancient lichens, themselves some of the earliest forms of life to creep over the sterile rocks, show their colouring after rain.

The volcanic rocks, where they poured down to the edge of the water and then cooled into solid shapes, do not seem to have changed their grotesque forms and patterns from the time when they were thrown as a molten mass from the bowels of the earth.

Heavy rains cascade down the sides of the cliffs, often penetrating into the nests of the sitting eiders. The eggs are chilled and the down soaked so that the birds have to desert and build again in a better position. The eggs are quickly pounced upon by ravens or gulls, for there is no wastage here of any sort.

Where there are patches of finely ground shells and rocks resembling a rough sand, ringed plovers have their nesting scrapes. They surround the nearly invisible eggs with a circle of white shell fragments, but make no other nest. On this beautiful camouflage the plovers must rely, as the gulls are on eternal watch for eggs and young.

When the plovers stand on thin legs amid a jumble of driftwood, dried dark seaweed, bright grey stones and the pale shade of the rough sand, they merge into the surroundings so well that only when they make quick forward runs can they be seen.

We nearly stumbled over a sitting bird as we trekked over the rocks towards the cliffs. The bird rose almost under our feet, and immediately began to try to lure us away from the site of the eggs. Although she had been so suddenly alarmed, she displayed no fear. Deliberately she paused after running a few yards and turned to make sure we were watching her. She then fell to the sand as if in real distress. Rising, she limped off among the rocks, dragging one wing as though it was broken. The actions were perfect and would have drawn most of her foes from the nest eggs.

We followed her between the stones as she limped ahead, always making sure that we did not come too close to her. Her behaviour was as realistic as it could be, and when she had drawn us away from her territory, the wing healed as if by magic and the little bird rose with a musically trilling call that echoed back to her mate watching anxiously from the top of a rock.

The eggs exactly blended into the mottled structure of the sand, and as we watched from a distance between the rocks, the female ran back lightly and silently to the nest and shuffled over the eggs for a moment to make sure they were all right. She also vanished against her background when she sat quite still.

To each of the many species that make these great bird rocks their summer home in the north, its own territory is all-important. Each pair of birds finds a site for which nature has best suited their colouring and habits. There is no part of the island, from the tide-edge rocks to the mountain peaks, which does not have its ordered place in the natural arrangement for survival and increase.

They are, indeed, the living rocks.

4 *Lonely Rulers of the Great Cliffs*

The lonely places of the earth over which the great brown wings of the eagles have flown for centuries have almost disappeared.

Two hundred years ago eagles were a common sight over Europe—in England, Scotland and the whole of Scandinavia. They soared over the sea and over the mountains and moorlands, the inland lakes and the coastline. Uncrowned kings of their domains, they had no real enemies. The time of the trap, the gun and the pollution of seas and lakes was still in the future, as far as a real threat to their existence was concerned.

From Iceland and Scandinavia in the west, to Mongolia and Kamchatka in the east; from Germany and Hungary, through Jugoslavia, Albania, Greece and Asia Minor, winged the sea eagles in their unfettered freedom of the air. In the European parts of Russia and into Siberia, as far north as the tundra zone, and then along the large rivers of this desolate region; ranging to lake Kola peninsula and along the Yenisei river to 72° N; this was the breeding world of the wide-winged, white-tailed sea eagle. And from its great soaring heights, as it wandered outside the breeding season, it could look down with its piercing black gaze upon the landscape of India or of China far beneath.

Many a coat-of-arms carried the eagle as a proud symbol of power. Untamed king of the sky, the eagle could be more careless in those days with its nesting sites. Then it had little of the distrust and fear of man that shows in the behaviour of the few eagles that remain in their free state today.

But the march of the hunter, the anger of the sheep farmer—combined with an obsessive hatred of any bird with claws and a hooked beak that swept throughout England, Scotland, Scandinavia and elsewhere in the last century, culminating in a price being put on the head of every eagle—began a destruction that has brought the eagles to the verge of extinction.

But not quite: while there remain the wild mountain peaks of such island groups as Vaeroy and other North Norwegian coastal bastions, the eagles have a last line of retreat. Here they can still be seen in their majestic silent circling flights, rising into the clear northern air until they are lost from sight.

Certainly eagles like an occasional lamb, as they do a reindeer calf, and a hare will fall victim to their claws, as well as a grouse, or a bird from the teeming millions of the nesting rocks. From the countless millions of fish in the sea and in the great lakes they also make their catch, but all the food they were able to eat was surely never enough to turn the hand of any man with a trap or a gun against them in a ruthless desire to rid the air of every eagle.

The sea eagle, the largest and most magnificent of the European birds of prey, with a wing span that reaches as much as 9ft, could formerly be seen flying over Scottish and English waterways in large numbers. Before 1871 it was reported that as many as forty could be seen together, attracted by carrion like a flock of vultures. But their days were numbered, for throughout the British Isles and Scandinavia a wave of killing reduced their numbers drastically in a few short years.

On the heather-covered slopes of the Scottish lowlands, with a mist dimming the distant vision, I have sat with an old gamekeeper who recalled with a sigh of regret that the last eyrie the sea eagles had used over Scotland was in 1911, and the last pair had left Skye, the final retreat in these waters, in 1916.

In the Scottish Highlands and along the banks of the lakes eagles had their favourite ledges and trees, used year after year. These sites were well known and gave the birds little protection when the sheep farmers turned their united wrath against the birds. One after another the old eyries were deserted as one or even both the parent birds were killed.

By the end of the eighteenth century the eagles had ceased to nest on the British mainland, and had taken refuge in the Scottish islands, where there were still many pairs. But the situation even there was to change so rapidly that by 1886 they were already scarce. Until 1815 the big brown wings would be watched over the Isle of Man, and even the bleak regions of Dartmoor knew them as breeding birds. The strong yellow claws, the murderous glint and set of the dark eyes, and the huge yellow hooked beak, gave to the eagle an appearance of a more ruthless killer than it deserved.

The hand of every sheep farmer, from Scotland to the Lofotens, was against the birds. On Skye a price of ten shillings was being paid for every eagle killed, at a time when the old trappers on Vaeroy were spending bitterly cold hours in their cramped pits to earn their three shillings a head. During the 1880s and 1890s the number of eagles trapped at Vaeroy, one of their most popular wintering islands, was enormous. One old trapper could take as many as 50 to 100 birds in the short period between October and Christmas, when the trapping was at its height. Two shillings of the money he received was 'head-money' and the third shilling was for the wing feathers, which were used for the making of excellent brooms.

It was not until the payment of head-money ceased that the interest in trapping lessened, and by then the birds had disappeared entirely from the Scottish scene, had been reduced to a small number of breeding pairs in Sweden, and drastically reduced in Norway.

Man suddenly turned an about-face and awoke to the fact that the wild life of the world needed the protection of law. The hunter hung up his traps and his guns as far as the eagles were concerned, but the path was not easy. In Norway there was strong opposition, especially from the island sheep farmers, until as late as 1968, to the sea eagle being put on the protected list of birds to be saved from destruction.

There still remain the illegal trappers, and those who seek out whatever eyries they can find and manage to reach, for the purpose of taking the eggs. Collectors are willing to pay handsomely for the eggs of a bird that is becoming ever more scarce, but even these dangers are not the chief cause of the great decline of the birds today.

The pollution of the waters by the discharge of oil and industrial waste has proven as deadly a weapon as any gun or trap. The eagle is the last link in the great nature chain that began with the microscopic algae, and when the waters of the lakes poison the fish, or the nesting sea birds are tainted with the pollution from the open sea around their rocks, then the eagles sit with patience upon eggs that contain no life. The tragedy is there: the lonely eagles, having found a last safe refuge from destruction by gun or trap, wait for young to hatch from eggs rotted with poison.

The pollution of the waters is not so great in North Norway as in so many other regions, and here, as in Iceland where they are reported on the increase again, the eagles have a chance for the future. But the position seems to be the reverse for their neighbours in Sweden. There the forests and lakes and long coastline gave a safe refuge for a great many sea eagles until a few years ago. Now, of the estimated fifty pairs that remain, the total number of eaglets successfully launched into the air at this time was *eight*, the lowest figure ever recorded. Of the twenty-four unsuccessful hatchings reported, some of the eggs had broken in the nest, believed to be due to the high content of DDT in the area over which the old birds flew. The position was similar in all the breeding sites. For the Swedish eagles there may be little hope for the future.

Perhaps the island on which we were climbing towards one of the old trapping pits can give the eagles a better fate. They are early nesters, laying their eggs in April when the cold winds bite at the exposed eyries and the warmth of the feathers of the female must constantly cover and protect them from the rawness of the air. She lays her eggs with an interval of several days between them, and as incubation commences from the laying of the first egg then there is also a difference in size between the two young that make their appearance after some forty days.

The wind blew with a cold bleakness on the May morning as we climbed upwards along one of the great slopes that rise from the centre of Vaeroy. From these slopes, first covered with rough vegetation, and then becoming bare as the grey rock rises higher to become jagged mountain peaks, there is a wide-ranging view out to sea.

Here, in an area greatly liked by the eagles, the old trappers had their lonely traps set into the side of the slopes. We knew that such a trap lay in our path, but the little dug-out had nothing to distinguish it from all the other grey stones that litter the mountain-sides.

When we eventually discovered it after a lengthy search, we had to pull aside the very heavy stone slab that formed the roof. This exposed the small pit into which the trapper had to climb in the darkness of the early winter mornings, drawing the slab over his head. It was necessary for him to conceal himself before there was light enough for the eagles to see his movements on the mountain-side.

I lowered myself into the pit and the slab was dragged across to make me a prisoner. The sense of being trapped myself was very strong. My head pressed against the heavy stone overhead and my legs were curled under me in a position that would have been

Page 51 (above) Vaeroy consists of 90-per-cent rock and calm days are unusual. Summers are cool with many storms; (below) only one house now remains inhabited in the once busy little fishing community of Mostad

Page 52 (above) 'The last of the Vikings': 85-year-old Monrad Mickelssen. He and his wife are the sole inhabitants of Mostad; (below) this puffin hound, a relic from the Ice Age with its six toes, is probably one of the rarest dogs in the world

difficult to maintain for the hours that the trapper remained in the pit.

The slope dropped away from the front of the trap, and I could see out through a narrow observation slit. On a farther slab of rock in front of the trap, a few yards away, the lure would have been laid to attract the eagle. This was a blood-smeared piece of meat, attached to a thin strong rope, which was passed through the opening slit so that it could be pulled in by the trapper.

It must have taken considerable strength of character on the part of the trapper to have got him out and along these exposed cliff slopes in the biting storm winds of winter and the darkness. When the snow covered the slopes, the luminous glow from its white surface would help him, but the way upwards would still be very precarious.

Once shut inside his small prison, the trapper had to wait with a patience acquired over the years of living on the island far from any distractions other than the natural elements.

As the light grew strong enough for an eagle to patrol over the slopes, eager for any food that might be found when the cliffs were bare of the nesting hordes of summer visitors and the fish swam deep, it would be attracted by the sight of the blood-stained meat far below. Alighting upon the bait, the great yellow claws would sink into the flesh, to hold on in a grip that was difficult to release. The big yellow beak would begin to tear at the meat, all thoughts of any possible danger forgotten for the moment. As the bird tore at the bait, so the trapper carefully and slowly pulled at the thin rope, drawing both bait and bird closer to the observation slit.

At the exact second when he felt the eagle was in the right position, the trapper would push his gloved hands through the opening, and grab the eagle by both legs. Keeping a firm grip, he was able to pull the big bird towards and then through the slit and into the tiny interior of the pit. The eagle was unable to use its wings in the confined space, and the trapper, with a skill

D

and courage that needed strong nerves, was able to give it a death blow to the head.

The method was not easy, as I could well imagine as I pictured the scene. Cramped as I was, the thought of fighting with a full-grown and powerful sea eagle inside the small pit, the sides of which almost pressed against me all round, was not one that aroused any enthusiasm. The three-shillings head-money seemed to me to have been well earned, though a good trapper could kill many birds in a single day, provided he kept well hidden inside the trap.

He could not expose himself to sight before darkness, or the trap would have been useless for the future, and the discomfort suffered by an old trapper must have been great. He dulled his cramped senses at times with the strong, clear spirit of the north, but a good head was necessary to pull in and dispatch a sea eagle, so drinking was not greatly indulged in for more than one reason.

For generations, as long as the oldest villager could remember from his own parents' talks, the sea eagles had patrolled the skies in large numbers over the humped hills of Vaeroy. With the coming of the darker days of autumn, which arrive very early in the north, many more eagles would arrive from the higher Arctic regions. 'The herald of the dark days' was an apt description, for the days are filled with a dull grey gloom in October, and the sun is entirely absent for some while.

There is one part of Vaeroy that nature designed for the nesting of the eagles, and for its companion of the isolated and sheer cliff faces, the raven.

From the heights on which the old trap was situated, we could see downwards towards and through a short deep valley. On either side rose the mountains and cliffs, dark grey when the sun was unable to penetrate into the valley. Boulders had rolled down the mountainsides during the years, to form huge massed piles. Their surface was no longer a pale grey, for lichens of various colours had gained a hold on them, blending the whole into a harmonious pattern that from above made the valley seem easier to negotiate than it eventually proved to be.

Small family groups of sheep and lambs wandered unchecked over the slopes from spring until late autumn, making the valley echo with an exaggerated sound as they dislodged stones in the scree. These gathered others around them to make miniature landslides, and the sound was heard from a long distance.

High over the rising, unclimbable cliff face, scarred and filled with deep cracks, we could see a pair of eagles winging in the slow circles that seem to delight them. They favoured one spot, coming down to perch together high on the mountainside.

The situation was ideal for an eyrie, and the old men of the village were sure the birds nested there but were uncertain of the exact spot. The valley was seldom visited except by the sheep, for the twisting and slipping path down to its floor was not one that now had any attraction. The eagles that once would have been the object of the trappers' close attention in winter flew unmolested along their lonely cliff face.

We had hoped to be shown a favourable spot from which we could study the birds at their eyrie, but after discussions with the fishermen we soon realised that we could expect little help with either finding the eyrie, or of ever reaching it.

On that first day high above the valley, sitting on the stone slab of the roof of the little trapping pit, we looked at each other and wondered what lay ahead for us.

Through the binoculars we could clearly see the big brown birds, with the sunlight catching at the wide white tails. They made an impressive sight, even at long range, and we felt the eager thrill of being at least this close to them. But the sight of the valley far below, almost in darkness, and the sheer rising walls of the cliffs on either side, with the sea showing in a gleaming white where one side of the mountain wall ended, left us in little doubt as to our problems. Somehow we should have to start going through the valley bottom, following the sheep path and carrying our equipment, until we came to within some reasonable distance of where the eyrie must be found overhead.

Hot and very tired, we arrived on our first morning of exploration of the valley at a point where the jumbled boulders and jagged rocks lay in a litter at the base of the cliff face over which the eagles soared. One of the birds was directly over us. As it was still quite early in the morning, the sun was striking the mountainside and showed every deep crevice as a hard black streak, giving to the whole face an appearance of harsh unfriendliness.

At our backs was the sea, glittering and calm on that morning in May, and as we watched the bird above us, the flute-like calls of several ring ouzels, mingling with the trills of a pair of oystercatchers gave us a little feeling of being less isolated.

It was obvious that the eagle pair had their eyrie on one of the many ledges that jutted out from the heights near the top of the cliff, but we had yet to locate its site. Eagles are usually silent birds, both in flight and in voice, and we knew we could not expect the same assistance from them as from the ravens in finding their nesting position. The whole while we had slowly and painfully traversed the floor of the valley, in a cold deep shadow, the deep croaking clanging voice of the raven had echoed between the valley walls. One of the big glossy black birds had followed us constantly, for in a deep crack into which the sun never shone and almost, as it later proved, under the ledge of the eagles, a pair of ravens had an untidy nest with five nearly fully-fledged youngsters.

As the eagle swung down from the top of the cliff to have a slightly closer look at the two small figures in the valley below, the raven pair immediately set up a chorus of alarm shouts and croaks that were flung back and forth between the cliffs. The noise and confusion that we were to witness many times commenced. The eagles uttered a series of sharp, high yelping barks, much too high and strained for such a fine bird, and with feverish energy the raven pair attacked them. They resembled a couple of black fighter planes in pursuit of big brown bombers, and twist and turn as the eagles might, they could not shake off these foes who bitterly resented their closeness to their young.

The croaking and yelping continued higher and higher into the still air above the tops of the cliffs. The four birds, for the female eagle had also left her eyrie and joined her mate, circled and twisted, gradually making for the open sea.

When the ravens felt the eagles were no longer a threat to their family, they dropped the chase and returned to the rocks. Why the eagles did not turn upon their pursuers and rend them in flight is difficult to know. I witnessed similar flights all summer, with kittiwakes, terns and gulls forming huge posses to attack a passing eagle, who either ignored all its attackers, or gave a high yelp of frustration or anger as it winged out to sea.

The early summer sun which had warmed the cliff face in the early morning rose higher. Soon it was behind the tops of the mountains, and at once a coldness gripped us as the face became a deep grey. It was the last we were to see of the eagles that day, and we cursed the ravens for their aggressive attacks. This was an added difficulty that we had not expected.

We retraced our steps back along the boulder-strewn track, climbing up the steep winding and slippery path made by the sheep on their way into and out of the deep valley. It was no easy task with our equipment, and we were forced to stop to recover our breath and strength many times before the level ground at the base of the trapping slopes was reached.

Later that evening, in the welcome warmth of the driftwood fire in our old rorbu hut, we relived in our thoughts the thrill of that first day. We ached with the strain of our efforts, and did not exactly relish the prospect of having to repeat this long and wearying trek back to the eagle cliff time after time. But we could see no alternative, and we decided to make an earlier start the next day.

The morning was grey, with a cold wind and a spattering of

rain. It was almost the end of May, and a cheerless outlook over the grey sullen sea. Dressing warmly, we again faced the wind in a dawn when it would have been better in the sleeping-bags, and began to climb the slopes near the old trap.

An underground stream had pushed up to form a small shallow pool high up on the slope. To this the eagles came often to drink and preen their feathers. We saw a mass of discarded feathers round the edge of the pool. Rocks littered the area in such an array that it was not difficult to conceal ourselves and shelter from the biting wind. We wanted to see if the pool was still being used.

After a wait of some half an hour, and with my watch face showing nine in the morning, the wide wings, with their out-stretched finger-tips, of the male eagle showed above the pool. The bird swung down to alight quite close to where we were hidden under the rocks. Taking its time, with its head feathers ruffled in the wind, it first drank from the grey water, then commenced a lengthy preening of its brownish feathers, taking especial care to pull each tail feather through the huge powerful beak.

Despite the cold and our cramped position, it was a fascinating experience to be high on the side of this slope, from which we had an eagle's eye view of the village and the sea far below, and watch this fine bird at its morning toilet. Here the eagles felt safe from all foes; here they had space around them in which to fly and hunt above the soaring peaks or the restless and still un-polluted sea.

Above the sound of the wind, whistling between the rocks which concealed us, came the deep croaking of the ravens and the warning 'go-beck, go-beck' cries of the willow grouse. The eagle stood motionless, almost invisible in the undergrowth, whilst its sharp eyes looked towards the grouse that flew with whirring white wings low over the vegetation of the mountain slope.

The calls of the grouse on the hills had an almost human in-tonation. This was the perfect landscape for birds that were lovers of the willow-streams, and thick matted heather and mixed cloudberry and blueberry undergrowth was ideal for their extremely well-hidden nests. When sitting, the hen, with her mottled brownish-red feathering, merged so well into her background that we should never have discovered a single nest had we not come close to treading upon a tight-sitting bird as we moved through the grasses.

With a harsh series of alarm calls the hen grouse would then rise and wing a short distance low over the heather, to land on a higher patch of grass. There she would remain until we had left the area of the nest. But with the ravens and the eagles constantly on patrol over the slopes, she would soon be back, invisible as she squatted over the large clutch of beautiful rounded eggs, with their pale background and mass of brown streaks and blotches.

The ground is very damp in such regions, and the grouse make a careful nest, hidden in a depression with a covering of leaves and grasses to conceal it even further, and lined with white feathers. With moderate luck, the slopes will have many families of grouse flying together in late summer, making the air resound with their deep, guttural calls.

The eagle tired of its preening. Silent of flight as ever, it rose without effort, allowing the wind to carry it upward on almost motionless wings, whilst it bent its head towards the ground and searched with a fierce penetrating look the slopes it knew so well. The grouse that had probably been frightened from the nest by another of the foes of the ground-nesting birds, either a stoat or a wild mink, had now disappeared again into the vegetation.

Gazing out to sea, with the whining wind stinging our eyes so that they misted over with tears in the cold, we could just see the mountain tops of the Lofoten range showing a pale blue over the water. On pockets along the summits were patches of snow, which remained all summer.

This was no day to spend in long, motionless watching, and already we were frozen after waiting in cramped positions between the rocks. With hands that hardly felt the dry vegetation we plucked from among the massed and matted mosses, blueberries and cloudberries, we gathered material for a fire. We always carried small thin pieces of birch bark for fire-lighting, which proved successful even in the worst of conditions.

The fire smoked abominably and our eyes were filled with a stinging lash that reminded me vividly of days spent with the nomadic Lapps in the farther north. But the water in our old blackened kettle was soon boiling. Never did the bubbling sound seem more welcome than on that bleak, cold grey morning high on the eagle slopes.

Around us the blueberries and cloudberries were already in bloom, and in late summer the harvest would be large of these delicious wild berries. Far beneath us were the nesting ledges of the kittiwakes, under which the angry swell pounded the base of the cliffs in a series of muffled, booming strikes. Even in the teeth of the wind, the plaintive wails of the kittiwakes reached us as they circled endlessly around their ledges.

We could search for the eyrie no more on such a day. Thankfully and slowly, for the slope was very slippery, we retraced our steps. Back in the rorbu we could listen to the wind. At least we had a fire, and fish, potatoes and home-baked bread to eat.

5 *Close to Disaster*

The last day of May was torn from the calendar. With June the sun and the warmth returned, but the wind was still a force that would not give us any respite from its caress. We arose very early on that first June morning, determined if possible to locate the site of the eyrie on the great lonely cliff face.

Shouldering our equipment, not without a deal of cursing on my part, we again faced the long and tiring trek through the bottom of the valley towards our base under the cliff. We knew now that the very early morning was the best time to arrive at our site between the big boulders.

Again the grouse whirred around us, and the ring ouzels watched us with great suspicion. Wheatears, wagtails and pipits all moved restlessly between the rocks, and out at sea large dark flotillas of guillemots and razorbills were drifting under their nesting cliffs.

It was a morning of calm beauty, but we wondered how long it would last. We did not have long to wait for a sight of the eagles. Against the deep blue of the now cloudless sky above the high sharp ridges, one of the pair suddenly appeared. Lit by the sun, the white tail gleamed in almost transparent brightness. In such conditions, with the light catching on the pale feathering of the head and neck, and the yellow of the claws and beak, the eagle seemed larger than ever.

She had taken no notice of us, it would seem, still and silent as we were far below. Settling on a grassy ledge, she proceeded to carefully preen the mottled feathering.

The colouring of the eagles was such that they were extremely difficult to watch for any length of time against their cliff background. The broken and blended shades of the cliff top made a perfect backcloth against which the eagles could remain motionless and almost invisible for hours at a time.

We presumed that there were now youngsters in the nest as the female was not sitting. She finished preening after a long and careful toilet. With a fixed position of the head, she remained still, gazing out over the glittering water. We strained our eyes to keep a watch over her movements. Eagles have such a silent flight, despite their size, that the slightest relaxation in observation can mean that the bird has disappeared over the top of the cliff, and the long watch has been in vain.

Soon the sun threw long shadows over the ledge and she became even more hard to distinguish from the rock at her back. When we thought we could concentrate no longer, the deeper brown form of her mate also appeared. Dropping quietly from the blue sky, it swept along the cliff face to alight suddenly on another ledge, where it remained for several minutes. Then it joined its mate, and together they rose, making a swinging turn over the cliff top.

Flying close together, wings almost unmoving, the back light of the sun now behind the cliffs catching at their feathering, they rose slowly in a picture of unhurried, untamed grandeur. The large bodies sat on the air as if weightless as they rose higher and higher in wide circles. Tired of this, they descended as quietly as they had soared upwards. They dropped to the ledge on which I had seen the male alight.

There were at this time no alarm shouts from the ravens. The eagles had not winged close enough to their nesting crack to annoy them sufficiently to go to the attack. There seemed to be an agreement between them that if the eagles respected their territory, the ravens would let the valley remain in peace.

Landing on the ledge together, the eagles were lost to our view for some moments. Through my binoculars it was now possible to see the ends of several sticks protruding over the edge of the ledge. Not daring to remove my gaze from this tiny spot on the great rearing face of the cliff, I watched until my eyes ached. We *had* found the site of the eyrie. This thought raced through my brain as I remained utterly still and concentrated on my watching.

Suddenly, silent as ever, the browner male eagle rose from the ledge. Claws hung down, showing the thick trouser-effect that the feathering gives to the legs, as it flew towards the sea. It dipped downwards, dropping into the water with a splash, and when it rose again, the drops of water from the feathers gleaming in the sun, its big claws firmly gripped a fish. With this it flew to a weed-covered dark rock on the edge of the water, settled, and proceeded to tug at the fish which was now still between the claws.

Silhouetted against the sharp glitter of the sun's rays on the calm water, the eagle stood out in sharp dark relief as it jabbed and pulled at its prey. After a short while it was joined by a hooded crow, looking very small and uncertain by the side of its huge companion. The crow hopped around the claws of the eagle, daring to also tug at the fish from time to time. The eagle ignored it completely, and the two continued to eat in what seemed to be perfect harmony.

The eagle rose, still bearing the fish remains, which it carried back to where its mate was still on the nesting ledge. Faintly, the cries of young reached us. We looked at each other with a pleasure mixed with worried wonder as to how we could ever reach this high, precarious ledge.

Both eagles left the eyrie, winging along the cliff face until they rounded a ridge and were lost to sight. After a few moments the sound of an enormous clamour of anger and fear reached us, indicating that the eagles were hunting among the massed kittiwake ledges, which were one of their favourite sources of food.

There was good cause for the eagles to be content with their summer life here. The site they had chosen was almost impossible to reach, and around them they had a larder that would give them a varied diet all summer, until their young could leave the ledge, at some ten weeks old, to begin their education.

The young ravens were now shouting lustily for food. The sun slowly swung round to again shroud the valley in a cold, deep blue shadow that made us shiver.

Sweetly and clearly the song of a wren reached our ears as we continued to crouch between the boulders.

In this lonely, windswept isolated northern valley, the tiny wren pair had flown to nest at the base of the cliff under the eagles. The legend of the wren, huddling among the back feathers of an eagle, being carried higher and higher into the blue until the eagle itself had reached the very pinnacle of its upsurging flight, came clearly to my mind. The wren of the legend had become the highest flyer of them all as it had flown from the eagle's back.

Certainly this tiny bird, with its jaunty tail and shrill powerful voice, showed great courage in choosing such a spot as this valley for its nesting. It was a very long way from the sheltered ivy-covered walls of an English garden, where I had long been accustomed to seeing the birds at their nesting.

We watched the small wren for some time with pleasure and affection. The contrast between it and the great eagles was even more marked in this great lonely domain made for the birds that prefer the uninhabited places of the earth. Why the wrens were there was difficult to know, but they brought a warming touch of home with their presence.

We had little idea of how we could reach the ledge high above for a closer study of the eagles. There seemed no way up at all for us. We were no experienced mountain climbers and, where the loose scree finished, the cliff face began to rise straight up. We examined the top of the cliff through our binoculars, but this gave us no help. The ledge was in a most difficult position, with the cliff face above it jutting outwards.

With an obstinacy that was unwise, we determined to return the next day with rope and make an effort to climb between the cracks to as far as we could. We should have known better.

An overcast, deep grey dawn greeted us as we rose at three the following morning. At four we were already on our way, trudging again along the unfriendly and slippery path at the base of the valley. Deep, thick, cold, grey mist covered the tops of the mountains. The cliff face itself was bleak and dark.

With us we had a fish, hopefully brought along with the thought that possibly we might be able to use it as bait to lure one of the eagles down to within a reasonable distance for filming. There was not a big hope, but at least we could try.

In the cold dawn light, with grey clouds making the sea a steel-grey sheet over which the puffins and the guillemots flew low, we placed the fish on top of a big dark boulder close to the cliff base, and retired to our hiding place between the rocks. We had by this time become expert at the building of stone hides, and there was plenty of material at hand from which to choose.

It was not one of the eagles that saw and came swinging down to our bait, however. The fish gleamed dully on the rock top, and we had not been in our hide for more than a few moments when the big glossy black wings of one of the raven pair flew around the rock, closely inspecting the fish.

The raven is one of the most suspicious of all birds, but it saw nothing dangerous about the fish after circling it several times, and eventually dropped on to the rock. With its huge gleaming black beak, the raven began to tear pieces from the fish. These it did not eat. Instead it took each portion and swung down to the rock-strewn ground around the boulder. With careful movements it pushed each torn-off piece of fish under a stone with its beak. Even in the midst of the summer plenty, instinct made the black bird save for future needs. Scrap after scrap was hidden in this way, despite the fact that the young ravens were shouting loudly for food from their crack in the cliff face. The raven eventually paused in its task to tear off a larger portion and wing back with this to the family. Before reaching the nest it gave a resounding 'korp, korp', and the noise from the young redoubled as it landed with the food.

For us it was a cold and damp wait between the rocks, and we knew now that we should see no eagle swing down to the fish. But over our heads the raven youngsters were emerging from the crack, to sit upon the edge of a rock, calling lustily the while. Flapping their wings in practice flight, they were watched by the old ravens, who shouted encouragement to them at intervals.

Soon the whole family of five youngsters were out of the nest, taking a first glance at the cold world around them. The raven pair would teach the young to hunt along the cliff face, the whole family keeping together for several weeks, until they finally disbanded in the autumn. Together they would wheel and twist above the cliffs, seeming to enjoy life to the full.

We must have been well hidden to have given the wily raven pair no cause for alarm, for normally it is almost impossible to get close to them. From a long distance they detect the slightest unusual movement, and immediately leave their scavenging along the coastline and rise in a protesting group.

The light gradually improved; the mist lightened and grew thin as a veil. From the sky above us holes were at last torn in the thick grey and depressing cloud mass, and patches of bright blue appeared. We were able at last to see to the eagle ledge. But this morning the ravens were in no mood to tolerate the eagles, and there began the familiar pattern of deep barking croak and answering high yelp as the four old birds began their chasing aerial acrobatics over the cliff top.

The ravens tired at last of the chase, and the eagles landed again, claws hanging down as they dropped towards the very highest peaks. From this great height they could survey their world below. As the mist swirled around them they became again invisible, but on such a day we thought we might have a reasonable chance of getting closer to the eyrie, if we could find a way up the cliff face by using the many cracks as foot and hand holds.

The weather that had showed promise of becoming warmer and brighter did not live up to that hope. Instead big sullen banks of cloud blew in from the sea and the wind rose. It was not now the kind of day to try our hand at cliff climbing, but we had made up our minds and had no desire to return to our base.

Our equipment was really more than we could manage, but there was no alternative but to get it along as best we could. Sheep had fashioned many small twisting paths during generations of wandering over the slopes to the heights. One of these we began to follow as it led upwards from the scree.

This scree, a collection of all the loose rocks and stones that had slithered down from the heights during many years, was itself a far from easy first stage to climb. Stones would slide from under our feet, starting small landslides that gathered momentum as they rolled to the valley floor. The noise was irritating to the nerves, as was the need to carry the film camera without cracking it against the rocks.

We gradually grew level with the deep dark crack in which the ravens had nested. At our approach, the entire family had flown off with shouts of protest.

To make matters worse, it suddenly began to rain: a thin misty rain that quickly turned all the boulders into slippery treacherous footholds that made our going much harder.

Ulla-Maija went ahead, more sure-footed than I, and as we went from crack to crack it became ever harder to swing the film camera on its tripod up to her. We paused, panting for breath, and surveyed the world beneath us. It was not an attractive sight, and as the rain was rapidly becoming more troublesome and the clouds a sullen mass of unfriendly heavy blue-grey, we decided we could go no farther. The camera had to be protected from damp, and we were getting wetter ourselves all the time. It was little use cursing at the weather; we had to save our breath for the return journey.

We had only climbed about one-third of the way up the cliff face, drawn upwards and given strength by the lure of what was on the ledge above us. Now that we were faced with the task of descending, however, the drop below us suddenly appeared terrifying.

I felt panic gripping me with the frightening fear that makes impossible any further movement up or down. I had known it before and knew that it would have to be fought, but when it takes control of the body then all the fingers want to do is to grip with all their strength at whatever rock crevices they are holding, and to remain pressed against the cliff face.

I called to Ulla-Maija.

'I can't move. You'll have to try to get down to just below me so that we can go down as close together as possible.'

My companion saw by the strained look in my eyes that fear now held me a prisoner in the crack to which I was clinging.

She began to climb down to me and had almost reached my side when the rock she was gripping began to break loose from the cliff face.

Gazing directly at her hand, I watched with a fascinated horror the rock slowly prising outwards. There was no time to release her fingers and try for another hold.

The rock came completely away from the mountain side, smashing to pieces on the rocks far below as it slipped from her fingers. Her feet slithered on the slippery surface, desperately searching for a hold for her boots. Suddenly she began to slide past me.

Page 69 (*above*) The Arctic skua, the feared pirate of the rocks; (*below*) the boldly marked skua's eggs are laid in the open with no pretence of a nest

Page 70 (*above*) The colourful wheatear; (*below*) shags stand motionless for hours unless disturbed

Under us was a sheer drop of several hundred feet with nothing to break the fall.

Her eyes were round and pleading, but fear held her silent as her fingers scraped frantically against the side of the cliff. The knowledge that her life now depended on some action from me released me from the panic that had held me a rigid prisoner on my small ledge.

With an action over which I had no conscious control at that instant, I shot out my right arm as she slid past me. Grabbing her jacket with the same intense grip with which I had just been holding on to the cliff face, I felt the strain of her weight pulling me away from the wall.

We were suspended for what seemed an eternity of time, my left hand holding as an anchor that had to hold us from falling. All feelings of panic had now left me; my only emotion was a cursing sweating determination to save us from a crashing fall to the rocks.

Ulla-Maija, fighting for her life, thrashed with her feet against the rock as she was swung back against its hard surface. Her left foot found contact with a small jutting rock, and I felt the weight being eased from my left arm. Placing her right foot against her left, she was able to press against the cliff, panting with weakness and strain.

For some time we remained perfectly still except for the pounding of our hearts and our heavy breathing. We had as yet no power to make any further move either up or down. Our eyes searched one another's, and slowly our lips eased into a smile as the mask of strain lost its tight grip on the face muscles.

Carefully and with infinite slowness we descended further. My left arm felt as if it had been pulled from its socket, and my fingers were swollen where they had gripped the sharp-edged rock.

At last we were able to slither down the scree, causing small landslides. Standing again on the muddy rocks at the base of the cliff in the deep valley, we began to shiver violently. We felt in no condition to remain longer in that lonely and damp spot

E

over which the wet mist now hung. But above all else we needed something hot to drink to ease the nervous shaking of our bodies.

Gathering small pieces of driftwood, we soon had a bright orange-yellow flame that rose higher and warmer as the wood burned fiercely. The heat caused our jackets to steam, but we huddled close to its welcome soothing warmth. Gradually, as we sipped hot steaming drinks, we began to relax.

We gazed upwards through the mist. The shelf of rock on which was the eyrie could be seen no more. The eagles had chosen their site well. Here they had lived and reared their young each summer in unmolested silence. Each autumn the villagers had been able to see the flights of the young eagles as they left the ledge with the parents.

We had found their eyrie but it seemed as if their intimate family life would remain a closed book to us, for the cliff was not to be climbed by us; of that we now felt certain.

One of the eagles came down low, to appear for a moment through the mist as it circled round us. It was so near and yet so far.

A sense of frustration lay heavily upon us as we sat in our rorbu that evening. Our clothes were drying in the heat from the wood-burning stove, but we felt now no real enthusiasm for returning to the valley. Somewhere we had to find a pair of eagles with an occupied eyrie to which we could come much closer. There was one old man to whom we could turn for help.

6 Saga of 'The Last Viking'

The calendar proclaimed it was 14 June, my birthday. From the rain-soaked window of the rorbu I looked out into the strong light of the sun. The wind was blowing hard and cold as usual. The decision had been made. We simply had to locate another sea eagle eyrie in a much more suitable position for filming and study.

Monrad Mickelssen was the man to question: old Monrad, 'the last Viking', as he was called by all the fishermen of Vaeroy and elsewhere in the chain of islands.

Along the jagged, broken and immensely long coastline of Norway are still to be found many old men who, in their thinking and adventurous way of life, resemble their long-dead ancestors, the Vikings. Mostly over eighty years of age, but still fit and active, they can recall the tough, unrelenting storms of the past that had to be faced in the open boats.

Norway has bred strong, independent men and women for centuries. But never in my travels among the villages of the north had I encountered a more clear-thinking, virile and likeable old fisherman than Monrad Mickelssen, who carried his eighty-four years with an ease that would have seemed suitable on a man many years his junior.

73

Our equipment was loaded into many packs around us. The fishing boat that was to take us over to Mostad dragged at its anchor with the pull of the wind and waves. Moving out of the quiet water of Vaeroy harbour, with its long arms of stone breakwaters keeping out the force of the waves, we were at once hit by both the wind and the white-tops, which crashed with a resounding crescendo of wild sound on the dark rocks projecting from the still shallow water.

As we plunged into the open sea the vessel rolled with a frightening frenzy. Standing at the doorway of the small cabin we had to grip the woodwork with both hands as tightly as was possible.

Spray shot over the bows in a thick mist, wetting us with a cold shower. Our great concern was to protect our equipment, piled on the deck. The deck itself was often awash as seas swept over it, to run back through the long slits along the deck sides. Thankfully we had placed everything as carefully as possible, for this was no pleasure trip, and was not the kind of day we would have chosen.

At last, and not before we both felt that sickness would completely overwhelm us, the restless seas smoothed as we entered the calming influence of the small natural harbour bay at Mostad. The water was too shallow to allow the approach of the modern fishing motor vessels, and the village would have had to die for this reason alone. In former days it had been filled with more than a hundred hard-working fishermen and their families. Then the open boats had been dragged from the swell at night by many willing hands.

From the sea, as we lay at anchor in deeper water, in preparation for loading our equipment into a rowing boat for the pull to shore, the village resembled a film-set that had been carefully built to represent just such a long-deserted outpost of the north.

Shells of the old fishing sheds remained, close to the shore rocks, turfed with a matting of thick earth and long grasses over birch strips. A profusion of wild flowers grew from the matted grasses of the roofs, and these now shook violently in the wind.

Within the sheds the ribs of rotting open boats showed as skeletons. Their keels were still sound and would withstand many more years of weathering.

Spread along the shore line were the empty houses with their windows and doors nailed up with wood. Standing alone, with its faded white paintwork clearly visible from a long distance, was the old school-house. At the farther end, close to the great cliff, old Monrad and his tiny wife had their own white house, standing firm against every winter storm close to the sea.

A thin strand of wire was carried on poles right round the bay to the telephone station at Vaeroy. Inside his house a very old-fashioned wall-hanging telephone kept him in contact with the outside world, as did a walkie-talkie outfit.

We had to make several trips with the rowing boat, landing everything at the end of one of the jetties that had taken such effort to lay in the shallow water. Each stone was flat and of great weight, and firmly fixed to the next by iron rods that were now rusty with much wetting from the sea.

The old school-house had formerly consisted of a large room, warmed by a tall round black stove in one corner, and furnished with uncomfortable, straight-backed benches for the pupils and a simple desk for the sole teacher. Now, however, all had been changed. Just in time for our stay on the island, the school had been transformed into several smaller rooms, suitable for housing the few hardy travellers who might wish to stay for a while.

There was no lighting, but this was not necessary in the period of the midnight sun.

Thankfully we carried the last of our equipment into the school. It had been a long drag from the boat, and we were not sorry to survey our small room, with its wood-burning stove and ancient oven, in which bread could be baked.

We entered the kitchen of old Monrad's warm wooden house by the sea. By the stove, glowing with its wood fire, his eighty-three-year-old wife busied herself preparing coffee. In honour of our visit they had opened up 'the fine room', which had the musty odour of a room long closed.

I had invited the couple over to the school-house for the evening, to celebrate my birthday with the cake that had not yet been made, but which my willing Finnish companion had promised *would* be made!

They agreed to come. He seemed as delighted as a schoolboy at having us in the village, and showed a keen enthusiasm for taking us to the bird rocks as soon as the weather permitted. About him was a vitality that was quite infectious and very stimulating.

As we sat on the straight-back chairs in the 'fine room', gazing round at the old family portraits, the two puffin hounds of which he was so proud came panting into the room. They sniffed eagerly around our feet. Almost the last of the race of ancient hunting dogs, with their unique six toes, they have been used for centuries on the islands to hunt and retrieve puffins from their nesting slopes. Regarded as a relic of the last Ice Age, they are now probably the rarest dogs in the world. The bitch looked as if life was becoming weary for her. Now thirteen years of age, she had produced twenty-eight puppies, many sired by the second dog, which was itself one of her puppies.

Small, very strong-looking, short-legged and with pale brown coats, the dogs were ideally built for the work they had done for so many years, when the hunting of puffins was at its height. The fishermen of Vaeroy did not use the nets on long handles that has been the traditional method of trapping puffins on other islands. They had probably never caught the enormous numbers annually taken by the fishermen of the Faeroe Islands, where up to half a million puffins have been taken season after season. On a normal day, the old fishermen and expert trappers on the Faeroes would kill between two and three hundred birds, but numbers up to nine hundred have been known when the puffins were in greatest supply. It is an amazing thought that, despite these great catches, the puffins continue to return year by year to their traditional nesting slopes.

From the kitchen came the odour of freshly cooked puffin. Monrad assured us puffins were delicious, as were young guillemots and shags later in the season.

The people of Mostad had relied on what nature could provide for most of their daily needs. From the sea came fish in abundance; from the sheep, meat and wool, and from the cows that formerly ranged over the slopes, milk. Berries in late summer gave valuable vitamins, and eggs and sea birds, preserved for the winter, gave an overall diet that was healthy and filled with variety.

Each July for centuries the hay has been cut. Around the rocks that cover the ground everywhere not a foot of space is ever neglected, for the hay is precious for winter feeding.

In the past the men had been poorly paid for their winter catches, with none of the modern fixed rates that make fishing a profitable business. Life had been hard, but for those like Monrad Mickelssen and his wife, it was also filled with a simple uncomplicated pleasure that had none of the stress of the urban community.

Seven children had been born to them in the village, without the aid of a doctor. Although they had now all drifted away to places widely separated along the Norwegian coast, they remained in close contact with the old couple left at the small outpost as guardians of the past. Eighteen grandchildren with twenty-four great-grandchildren: these were the figures that Monrad proudly gave us. His eyes twinkled with pleasure as he felt among the papers in old drawers to find faded photographs showing not only the family members, but the old open boats in the background. In carefully posed groups the men were gathered around the big barges used to transport the fish down to Bergen, a long distance from the Lofoten range. Eagerly the return of the barges, with payment for the sold hard fish and perhaps the purchases that had to be made in the city so far away, was awaited. At times the wait was very long, for the barges were at the mercy of the weather on their long trips southwards.

As had happened in the villages all along the Lofotens in the days of their infancy, one family more enterprising than the others had opened a small shop. Even in a poor community there were items that had to be bought, and the shop-keepers had usually prospered well.

Close to the school-house stood the shuttered remains of what had been the village shop on Mostad. And with the shop had followed the school, for the numbers of children of school age had risen to some twenty-five at the period when the population of the village stood at a hundred and twenty. The bell above the white wooden walls had clanged in many years of fierce winter storms, unprotected as the building was at the edge of the sea.

At that time a rough roadway had run through the little outpost, and those who dreamed of connecting Mostad to Vaeroy by road instead of by boat had worked out plans for the laying of a road running right round the great bay. It was indeed an ambitious plan in the age of much more primitive equipment for road making. But the men were tough and strong of arm as well as obstinate of head. The roadway had been commenced, snaking out in a tiny thin ribbon along the shoreline.

Using the primitive tackle with which they had shifted the heavy grey slabs forming the small jetties that held back the worst of the storm winds from the village, the fishermen had persisted in their roadmaking. During the summer months, when the great shoals of cod had departed from their waters, there was time for such work, which had been undertaken willingly and without thought of payment.

Perhaps the energetic builders never allowed their thoughts to travel farther along the road than the length they had managed to level. If they had they would probably have been daunted by the labour that lay ahead. How it would finally have been overcome will never be known, for the road now ends abruptly, close to where the sheep track and narrow path rises up and along the sheer edge of the big bird cliffs with their nesting puffins. The village was to remain isolated, but it was also destined to die.

With the coming of the motor vessels and the need for giving the children better schooling, the villagers were faced with the choice of remaining to eke out a precarious existence with their children at school away in Vaeroy, or of leaving their homes to the fate of the seas and the winds.

At a mass meeting in the school-house it was eventually decided to abandon the village. Monrad recalled the low spirits with which the villagers nailed up their doors and shuttered their windows. On a bright summer morning they had left in their fishing boats, watching from the open water as their home under the great dark cliff grew smaller in the distance.

On the shore rocks two lonely human figures had remained: Monrad Mickelssen and his wife. By their side were their puffin hounds. The outside world offered them no attraction.

We left the house at the base of the sheer cliff face, along which so many guillemots and razorbills were later to make the air resound with their growling calls from the high nesting ledges. The old roadway was now a narrow track, filthy with the droppings of many sheep that used the path daily on their way to the slopes.

The low walls of rock slabs that had kept the sheep from the hay still surrounded the small fields. Wheatears and ring ouzels watched us curiously. There was no other sound at that moment except the whistling of the wind between the boards of the old sheds.

Gathering as much driftwood as we could carry, we returned to the school-house room, and felt thankful to have this refuge. Our water had to be fetched from the tap close to Monrad's house. It was the only supply in the village. But when I brought back buckets of water, the cheering sight of grey smoke rising from the chimney of the little white house greeted me as a welcome sign of home. It was the first time for years that the chimney had felt the warmth of the smoke, and we felt that perhaps the old school-house was glad to have life in it once more.

Our room was soon warm from the heat of the driftwood,

smelling strongly of the sea. Ulla-Maija opened the oven door many times to feel its temperature with her hand. She had to judge when it was ready to take the cake mixture.

By the early evening the small table was laid. The cake was newly baked and its appetising aroma filled the room.

In the cold wind of mid-June, I walked back along the slippery path to meet our guests. The elderly pair were slowly walking through the village they knew so well, facing the elements of their northern world.

We sat around the small table. The school-house revived many memories for both Monrad and his wife. The wind had gathered even more force. The sun had long since disappeared behind the towering cliff, and we were in a cold deep shadow.

Monrad praised the birthday cake. Like all the old fishermen of the north, he appreciated greatly a woman who was able to fend for herself under most circumstances. Quickly Ulla-Maija had won her way into his affections, and he showed it in his twinkling blue eyes.

We began to ply him with questions about the possible nesting site of the eagles that patrolled the skies over the Mostad cliffs.

We had expected that he would undoubtedly know the exact location of an eyrie, but disappointingly he explained that he knew they nested somewhere up in the range of mountains behind Mostad, but he could not pin-point the position. He wanted to show us the nesting ridges of the sea birds: the narrow and difficult ledges to which he had himself been lowered as a boy in search of eggs. If we were lucky enough to find the sea eagles during our search, then he wished us luck. We should need it if we were ever to get close to them. This was cold comfort for us, but we had to be content with it.

Monrad could relate stories of the eagles sweeping down, seven at a time, to within a short distance of his fishing boat in winter. Hunger lessened their fear of man, and in any case they knew Monrad well by sight and had little cause for alarm at his closeness. The fish he could throw to them were seized with no sign that the great birds were embarrassed or ashamed to be taking food in this lowly manner. But, as soon as the early spring arrived and the mating urge came upon the mature birds, then it was impossible to approach them. Keen of eye for every movement below, they would not disclose their nesting ledge easily to our searching gaze, he assured us. Their natural and deep-rooted distrust of the two strangers in the village would probably keep them at a greater distance than usual from the sheep path by the wall of the cliff.

Late that evening, after the old couple had returned to their home and the glow of the midnight sun was caressing the slopes of the cliffs behind their white house, we watched the sea eagle pair wheeling and twisting high over the cliff top at the rear of the school-house. The cliff top was filled with the activity of a great number of razorbills and puffins. Every now and then one of the razorbills would fly high over the school, wings making a high screaming sound that exactly resembled a projectile fired from a cannon.

We were reluctant to creep into the sleeping-bags. The desire of the northern Norwegians to remain up and about at almost all hours of the summer was understandable. They wished to enjoy to the full every hour of the light, in preparation for the long dark autumn and winter ahead.

We began our exploration of the cliff face the next morning. The slippery sheep path, which was the only track along the wall of the cliff, rose higher above the sea. The cliff face was broken and scarred by countless small cracks and crevices, from which wild flowers and patches of grasses poked in profusion. It was an ideal place for puffin tunnels, and from time to time large parties of the birds came racing in, wings whirring at a furious rate, from a fishing expedition far out.

The weather was very dull with a cold wind that later blew in rain. We sheltered at the top of the sheep track, before it dropped once more downwards. Here there were no trees, apart from a stunted rowan ash or two, whose qualities of survival we had long since learned to appreciate.

The water far below us was calm and littered with great black and white patches. These were where the guillemot and razorbill flotillas, mingling with the puffins, rode the swells for hours at a stretch. The groups constantly changed shape, drifting along with the tide. The water here was rich with food, and they had no cause to exert themselves. As yet they had no young, and the days could be spent quietly swimming and fishing.

Oystercatchers had apparently divided the whole length of this rocky coastline along the bay into sections. As soon as we left the domain of one pair, another pair would take up a series of far-echoing alarm calls as we trespassed into its territory.

As we rounded the end of the line of cliffs, swinging into the northern edge of the island, the wind hit us with a bite that almost took our breath for a while. Bent into the wind we trudged along, amid the piles of driftwood and poles, towards the caves and ledges where the kittiwakes had their main nesting sites.

Kittiwakes perched on the dark rocks in their thousands. The mist from the spray covered them as they hunched facing into the wind. Without warning the whole cloud would rise as one, and swing upwards with a massive chorus of wailing cries that were made more plaintive by the roaring of the breakers.

Hidden close to one of the huge boulders we were unobserved by the sea eagle that swept down and caused panic among the nesting ledges as it swung along the cliff face within touching distance of the sitting birds. Not a bird remained on the eggs. The whole cliff face seemed alive with white flashing wings as the kittiwakes went to the attack. In the heart of this violent mob the wide brown wings of the eagle carried it twisting and turning upwards, whilst it gave a sharp yelp of anger and irritation. One of the great advantages of the huge colonies was the protection that each bird would give to the other by their closeness.

But the eagle was looking for sickly or dead birds, which it pounced upon instantly. A bird falling sick received no sympathy from its neighbours, who attacked it with vicious pecks until it managed to struggle away to a rock by itself. There, bleeding and helpless, it was an easy prey for the eagle. It was rare indeed to find a complete dead bird. Skeletons that lay among the rocks had been picked clean. There was no wastage, for the ravens, the eagles and big black-backed gulls acted as efficient cleaners of the cliffs.

The days passed and the storm winds seem to increase in force, holding us almost prisoners in the school-house which creaks in the gale.

The old turf roofs hold, as they have done for generations, with their wild-flower gardens blowing furiously. Behind the sheds the tops of the mountains are invisible because of the thick swirling grey fog. It is cold and there is a sullen greyness in the landscape that is only relieved by the flashing bright black and white of the oystercatchers. Their colours seem to glow, especially the long orange beaks, as they fly round and round close to the school-house.

Monrad does not let the storm winds stop him from planting

his potatoes in a small patch close to his house. The two dogs never leave his side as he digs out the small trenches for the seed potatoes, the wind tugging at his thin frame. He greets me with the same pleasure as always when I push into the wind to fetch water from his tap. Drops of water drip from the end of his nose as he pauses in his work and shouts to me to follow him. He wants to show me his new boat of which he is justly proud.

Drawn up on the primitive little slipway that he has constructed himself, the pale brown varnish of the boat smells of newness. It has an outboard motor, now carefully wrapped, and as soon as the weather improves, Monrad is anxious to show us his skill along the dangerous channels at the base of the cliffs. Gazing into the sky, he screws up his eyes and hopes that the next day will be fine.

In the late afternoon, sweeping in with the steel-grey high tide, comes the rain. It rattles on the windows of the school-house, and the whine of the wind is more persistent than ever. Only a few eiders brave the waters between the rocks close to the shore.

7 *Struggle for Survival*

The bad weather continues and Monrad is as yet unable to launch his boat because of the dangerous currents around the rocks that jut into the sea at the base of the cliffs.

The sun manages to glitter for a time on the grey water of the bay. At this time the sea is never empty of birds, swimming and diving in huge massed flocks. Effortlessly they ride the small waves in the light that is never absent at this period of the midnight sun.

Under the dark caves, over which the kittiwakes have their countless closely packed nests on the lines of ledges, nest a colony of black guillemots. Deep under the stones they have laid their attractive eggs, hidden from the winged foes over them. Lovers of the closeness of the spray and the waves, their favourite perching and gathering rocks are at the very edge of the breakers.

The black guillemots have little fear of man, and by careful movements so as not to disturb them we were able to approach very close to the groups that either sit or stand engaged in what seems to be a long and earnest conversation. They face each other, the thin black beaks almost touching, and open very bright red mouths as they nod their heads seriously. From them comes only a thin wheezing sound that is quickly lost in the roar from the waves.

When they are forced to fly, on their black wings with the showy white patch, the coral red webbed feet splay out behind them, held high close to the body. Just above the waves they fly, fast and light. They prefer to remain close to the coast all year if possible, taking their fish from the weed-filled water up to about 25ft deep, but they can dive to a great depth if necessary. They have none of the clamour of the kittiwakes; none of the massed flights of the puffins, but a toughness that is unequalled except by the ravens.

Where the winds whistle over the high Arctic landscape close to the North Pole in the depths of winter and when other birds have long since flown south, the black guillemots can be found in the open cracks in the ice. While most of the adults fly south, or stay in the area of the nesting rocks, many young black guillemots remain in the coldest regions. They require very little open water in order to survive, being able to dive into the cold dark depths of the ocean. They have always appeared to me to be too delicate for such a winter struggle to survive, but they have remarkable powers of endurance. The accumulation of fat that the black-downed youngsters grow around their bones during the forty days they are fed in their underground hiding places serve them well all winter.

They have none of the desire to gather and nest in huge colonies that is shown by the guillemots lining the ledges high above them. Where the rocks jumble together to make a number of suitable deep cracks, then several pairs will nest close together; otherwise single pairs take over any dark crack that suits them, irrespective of whether they have near neighbours or not.

The black guillemots, sitting in the late evening, darkly silhouetted against the glare of the sun just above the horizon, make one of the most charming sights of the northern world.

When the weather is very bad, as it now continues to be for days on end, there seems to be even greater activity along the top

Page 87 (above) Guillemots often nest in long rows close to each other; (below) sometimes they prefer to build under overhanging rocks where the eggs are better protected

Page 88 (*above*) Eider ducks, almost invisible between the rocks, rarely leave their eggs during incubation; (*below*) newly hatched oystercatchers, beautifully camouflaged to match their surroundings

of the great cliffs. The mist makes our faces damp as we gaze upwards, and the air has a dismal cold rawness that penetrates our
warm clothing.

The puffins swarm around on the heights almost as though
they were in panic flight. They have the greatest difficulty in
landing on the wet rocks, red feet slipping and sliding as they
touch down. Time after time they make circles in preparation for
landing, only to change their minds at the last second. A second
or even a third attempt is necessary, and because of this there is a
constant whirring mass of wings and small black and white bodies
around us.

When they do gather in family groups outside their tunnels or
on their rocks by the sea, they bow to each other in a curious
dignified manner. They have no wish to be alone at any time it
seems, although two will sit outside a hole watching the never
ending spectacle around them. Then, as though infected by the
others, they too take off again with a high whirr of the small
wings, dropping rapidly towards the sea.

From the birds outside the holes comes a guttural sound that
reminds me of the creaking of a rusty gate hinge. The high slopes,
a mixture of broken rocks and earth into which the birds can
tunnel, using their huge flattened beaks as efficient shovels, seem
alive with puffins. When the mist rolls away from the heights
they come into view like a huge swarm of dark bats against the
greyness of the sky. Here on Vaeroy is one of their greatest strongholds in the north.

They seem unpredictable in their movements. On some days
huge flotillas ride the waves near the rocks, the sun catching and
gleaming on their white breasts, and on others at the same hour
the water is empty of them.

Of the several million that wing back each season to the cliffs
where they were hatched, a great many are immature birds, not yet
ready for mating. Time seems to hang heavy for some of these
youngsters, but they are always willing to help out with the
incubation of the single white egg that is laid so far into the

F

earth. The rightful owner of the egg can often fly off for a long period in search of food, but during this time the egg is warmed by one of several birds who seem to form a group around every nesting hole. The incubation period is quite long, about forty days, but the old birds are not so bound to their underground prisons as are the sea eagles on their lonely eyries. With so many helpers, there is constant activity along the tunnel as first one bird and then another will take a turn at sitting.

From early dawn until about ten in the morning there is a quietness around the huge colonies that soon changes as the puffins begin to return in big flocks from their fishing expeditions. Then there is life indeed both on the water under the cliffs and around the nesting slopes, and the whirring flights to and from the holes continue until late evening, when there is again quiet.

The soil around the holes, made rich with the nutriment from their droppings, is a wild garden of many colours that is a delight to see at this time of the year, despite the depressive mists.

Some distance above the sea and right under one of the favourite perching rocks of the puffins, a pair of oystercatchers have two newly hatched young on a large flat stone. The old birds are trying to get the youngsters down to the sea, but the small birds show little desire to move in the cold weather. They would remain huddled close to the showy female, but she is impatient to get the chicks to a safe, less exposed spot. Eagles, ravens, black-backed and herring gulls, as well as Arctic skuas are all waiting for the chance to pounce on any young left in a position where they can be seen, and the adult pair of oystercatchers know it and are very nervous.

Both the parents call anxiously, and as the first of the young comes to the edge of the stone the female alights close to the tiny shivering figure on its long legs. She gives it a deliberate push over the edge, sending it sprawling to the rounded grey stones of the shoreline below. The chick, stunned for a moment, soon struggles up on unsteady legs and runs towards the male, standing on guard on the top of a rock and calling the whole while.

The female repeats the action of pushing the other chick over the edge, slipping after it herself, and the small family gather together in the sheltered spot by the edge of the sea where they will remain while the young are being taught to fend for themselves.

Their actions have been watched by a group of about twenty puffins on the white-topped rock above them. Two black-backed gulls, eyes unblinking, also watch from a nearby rock jutting out of the sea. Their cold merciless glance sees all that happens along the cliff face. Whereas the raven soars along the face, and the eagles make long gliding swings back and forth along the ledges, the black-backs always seem to be close at hand wherever eggs and young of the lower rock-nesting birds are to be found.

From the moment the eggs of these teeming millions of birds that inhabit the bird rocks all summer are laid, the struggle for survival commences. Winter and summer, through the storms and blizzards of the northern waters, the armies of nesting cliff birds will strive to reproduce enough young to carry on the species in a constant flow. The losses are enormous, and it is truly remarkable that there remain today the numbers that make so many of the great bird rocks of the far north a mass of life all summer.

A vast number of the sea birds are shot or trapped annually. In Greenland the shooting of the auks, especially the guillemots, has seen a steady diminution of the birds by many hundreds of thousands each winter, and the black guillemots have also been ruthlessly hunted. An estimated fifth of the great flocks gathered around the Greenland southern coastal waters have been killed for food. Kittiwakes do not winter as far north as some species, but many thousands are killed in winter by the villagers of the Newfoundland coastline, where their flesh is preferred to that of all other birds. They are easily lured to where they can be shot or trapped.

It has always been the traditional thinking of the men and

women who live close to the sea that the fish and the birds are
their birthright, to be taken in as large numbers as possible. The
thought that possibly these great flocks of birds might one day
diminish in size has never entered into their calculations when
collecting the eggs, taking the youngsters or trapping the birds in
winter.

Man himself has probably been their worst enemy, but he has
a willing band of feathered and furred assistants who have waged
a never-ending war on the birds of the huge cliffs. Rats, brought
ashore in many instances from a washed-up wreck, have played
havoc among the nesting colonies of some of the puffins, who
have enough to cope with from their other foes.

In southern Greenland, where the villagers keep a large sheep
population, the glossy ravens themselves have had a bounty placed
on their heads. There they are also much liked as food, but are
certainly not the easiest birds to kill when they have grown adult
and wily. The youngsters, however, are more easily taken,
especially when food is scarce in midwinter and they gather
round the piles of excrement and waste left out near the villages.

Around the great cliffs of Vaeroy and Röst the raven population
does not vary to any great extent from year to year, although
each pair seems to produce a good batch of young in the early
summer. The cliffs could support a much greater number all summer when there is food in plenty, but by instinct the ravens divide
up the cliffs into sections, each ruled over by a single pair. Winter
is a critical time for the ravens, who can, however, exist on the
most meagre of rations; and, as they have no great wish to migrate
from their chosen cliffs, it would mean a less rewarding search for
food in winter if the summer population grew too large. The
youngsters, who fly with such ease with their parents for several
weeks of late summer, are driven off in autumn to fend for themselves, and, although some of the old birds do fly farther south,
most remain all winter on the cliffs, scavenging food where they
can find it.

Whilst we are waiting for the mists to clear a little so that we can begin the search for the eagles, we have a chance to study the life of the eiders, terns, common gulls, plovers, wheatears, pipits, and the other birds that find their summer home among the spray-wetted rocks by the edge of the tide. It is a fascinating world, but these shore-loving birds are not left in peace for a moment. They have to fight to survive as much as any of their neighbours nesting high above them.

Like sooty-winged bats of the daylight, a pair of Arctic skuas wing over a small flock of sheep as we watch the low rocks from a distance. We come nearer and at once the skuas cease their patrolling and turn their attention to us. Delicately they weave over and close to our heads, then settle a few yards away on a rock.

They are not attractive in colouring, these two being an all-over sooty brown-black. There are others of the same species that are half white, and on the flat marshlands at Röst there are many pairs nesting around the small pools. With their two long protruding tail feathers, and their finely built bodies made for speed of flight, the skuas are relentless in their pursuit of tern or gull.

The kittiwakes, too, are harried by them day after day. Being as relaxed and graceful in flight as they are, the skuas have little difficulty in following the twisting and turning of a kittiwake or tern, in the hope that the bird will eventually disgorge what food it has in its efforts to escape. The skuas seem to have no desire to fish for themselves, being content to rob the birds that have worked hard for their catches. They have infinite patience as highway robbers, but they could just as well catch their own fish, having a speed equalling that of the terns. They represent yet another foe to the nesting birds, ready to steal eggs or early young, and their own two eggs are laid among the rough grasses in a careless manner with little pretence at nest building.

They had suddenly arrived, this pair we were watching, late enough for all the other nesting birds to have eggs. Where the skuas come from is little known, for their winter life is something of a mystery. They often nest in very large scattered colonies, but out at Vaeroy we saw them only as single pairs. The pair obviously had eggs close to us. One of the birds tried the instinctive trick of playing at being hurt in order to draw us from the spot. She was very good at it, flopping down almost at our feet and dragging herself over the ground with a most realistic imitation of a bird with a broken wing. From her wide open beak came a series of weak calls, encouraging us to think she was exhausted. My admiration for her as an actress was great, and we followed her for a time to see where she would lead.

When she felt she had lured us far enough, she rose without effort into the air and both birds circled gracefully around our heads, coming very close and peering at us with their dark eyes in a fearless manner. On the top of a grassy mound were the two eggs, closely resembling those of the common gull, and difficult to see in the grass.

Among the jagged clutter of low rocks by the water under their domain were the eggs of the common gulls, who nested as a colony at this spot. Many were from a second laying, for the early eggs had already been taken by the villagers and the greater black-backed gulls. The number of broken shells were silent witnesses to the ones the black-backs had eaten. The body of one of these big black and white robbers lay close to the nest of the skuas, and had itself been picked clean of flesh by the beak of the sea eagle. Eat or be eaten was the rule by which the life of the cliffs and rocks here was controlled.

Like the black-backs, the skuas knew where most of the eggs of the low rock birds were to be found and the skua pair kept a special watch over the eggs of a pair of oystercatchers that nested quite close to them. Each time the skuas flew silently over the nesting site, the male oystercatcher would rise with a penetrating protesting shout, to be followed by its mate rising from the eggs to join in the chorus of anger. At other times she would sit quietly, long orange beak pushed between the back feathers, eyes closed whilst the male remained on guard on a tall rock nearby.

Around her the males of the common gulls and the Arctic terns also stood on watch whilst the females incubated the eggs. At times when peace reigned over the rocks, it was a sight of attractive beauty, but the mere glimpse of a passing raven, eagle, black-backed gull or skua was enough to cause confusion and near panic among the birds that had been so peacefully sitting on their eggs a moment before.

The eggs of the oystercatchers were on the point of hatching. At intervals the female would rise, give them an impatient jab, and then shuffle them into a more comfortable position. Once she walked away from them, only to return at the first sign of enemy life overhead.

The sighing of the wind was the only sound at times over the low rocks, and we ourselves felt like dozing in our shelter between the boulders. But the second the eagle came into sight from the mist overhead, dropping low in its patrol over the water and rocks, then the air erupted with noise and wings. The cries of the gulls mingled with the cloth-tearing screech of the terns and the kleeping calls of the oystercatchers.

The concerto of the north, of which nature itself was the composer and conductor, continued without a break. The following day the breakers crashed with a vicious smash on the low rocks, covering the sitting birds with white spray.

Over the rocks, battling with the wind with feathers ruffled, flew the ravens. One flew down to alight close to where a pair of ringed plovers had their two eggs well camouflaged among the finely ground stones that made a rough sand. The female plover left her eggs and ran on her long legs up the slight slope to where she could jump on to a rock and observe her black foe, who had sunk from sight between two boulders.

The raven, however, was only interested in the white body of an Arctic tern that had suddenly stopped in mid-flight and had dropped like a stone in unexpected death. The raven had detected it at once, following the body down as it landed between the rocks. Now it sat astride the dead tern, pulling pieces from the still-warm bird.

The ringed plover watched intently from the top of her rock, a trim little figure in the midst of such a restless world. Satisfied that no harm was intended to her eggs, she returned and shuffled over them, at once becoming almost invisible as she blended into her surroundings.

Despite the wildness of the weather, the eggs of the oyster-catchers were breaking open to disclose the wet struggling forms that would soon dry into attractive chicks. The female protected the youngsters as they broke from the eggs, shielding them against the spray and the fierce winds.

Instinctively, as soon as they could take their first faltering steps, they would hide at the warning call from the parents. Pushing into the nearest grass clump, or one of the many cracks between the rocks, they would remain still and motionless until the threatened danger was past. Camouflaged with down, their survival at this early age depended on their ability to merge into their surroundings so that even the keen eyes of the gulls or ravens would miss them.

The Arctic skuas came down to the attack as soon as they knew the youngsters were hatched. They were met by a furious onslaught from the parents, who were thoroughly roused by this intrusion into their family life. They would have attacked almost any foe at that moment. The skuas, graceful in flight as ballet dancers, were reluctant to acknowledge defeat, however, and the battle raged over the nest site for some time. One of the skuas did eventually land close to where the two chicks were hidden in a crack surrounded by flowering sea pink, but it was immediately chased off by the old black and white birds.

The skuas broke off the battle for the time being. They would wait and try again, but I felt they had little chance of success against the oystercatchers, who are always excellent parents and keep a sharp watch for danger.

Two or three days later, as the weather began to improve, we returned to the low rocks to survey the scene. Many of the eggs of the terns and the common gulls had hatched. But of a large number of fluffy youngsters there was no sign. The black-backs and herring gulls, together with the ravens and the skuas, had snapped them up. Only a very few hid from sight between the rocks.

The situation was different with the oystercatchers, however. The young were now being taught to bathe by the female. Choosing a very small pool of water that had gathered between two or three rocks, she walked into this, bent down and threw water over her head and back with a great show of splashing and shaking of the feathers. Her mate remained on guard close by. The two young watched her for a while, fascinated by all the splashing. Then one, followed by the second chick, walked unsteadily into the pool and tried to imitate each move of the parent. Dipping tiny wing stumps into the water, and almost toppling over in the attempt, the chicks persevered, ducking small heads under the surface and rising to allow the drops to roll off their bedraggled down.

It was a scene of wild education that could not have been seen to better advantage. The peace was short-lived as normally among these rocks.

Another enemy, slim and deadly as a tawny shadow of evil, carefully crept between the stones, ever closer to where the family were bathing. As the stoat moved slowly forward, its small dark eyes were fixed with grim concentration on the chicks. Once in a good position, the killer began to wriggle its hindquarters in preparation for a sudden lightning pounce. At that moment it was noticed by the male oystercatcher. All bathing was forgotten in the rush to attack the stoat. The youngsters pushed quickly into a crack near the tiny pool, water seeping from their wet down, and the stoat retired defeated.

The stoat and the wild mink, as well as a few sea otters, were an added menace to the birds. Mink had escaped from the mink farms dotted about the Lofoten range, become wild, and had managed to breed. Immensely cunning, they matched their skill against the watchfulness of the birds all round the coastline of the island.

Very few of the youngsters hatched after the long days of incubation could hope to remain alive until the autumn migration flights. The percentage of survival was very small, for the enemies of the birds were many.

This northern region did not mean an easy life for the birds. The sea eagle and the guillemot youngsters faced the rains in the open, the drops rolling from their feathering as they hunched against the weather day or night. The eggs of the black guillemots would be washed out of their holes by the high tides, and those of the low rock birds taken by a host of foes.

The fight to survive was constant, never ending, just as it has always been through the countless years that birds have existed. Left alone, however, the scales would balance each season. But with oil and poison also weighed against them, the plight of some of the birds was fairly acute. Elsewhere man has threatened to destroy by pollution the careful natural balance, maintained century after century, but in the clear and mostly uncontaminated seas around the great rocks of Vaeroy and Röst the birds still have a chance to survive.

The mood of the island seemed to have settled over us. Patience was to be the main virtue against the summer weather that showed us so little of the sun. We could not fight the elements; we had to learn something of the philosophy of Monrad, who, whatever the weather, could gaze into the evening sky and half-promise a fine day on the morrow.

8 *The Sea Provides for All*

Monrad Mickelssen was eager for us to explore the great broken impressive cliffs that rise directly from the sea to protect the village of Mostad. We have to round the small bay and then face the force of the open water that is seldom calm. Only in the calmest of days can a landing be made along the cliffs, and because of this the birds there have an unmolested life as far as human intrusion is concerned.

He was prepared to launch his new boat, fitted with its gleaming motor, despite the growing wind and the grey water. The early morning had been very calm, and he judged that the swell that had smashed against the base of the cliffs for so many days had now subsided enough for our trip.

A haze of thin cloud began to obscure the face of the sun, which had given such an encouragement to us. The wind had again freshened the sea and immediately the sharp bows of the small open boat dipped into its heavy grey-green mass sheets of spray shot over us. There was no shelter on the boat, and my thoughts were concentrated on protecting my equipment.

I looked at the old man intently to see his reactions. It was with real misgivings that I had set out, but Monrad did not seem to share my fears. As I gazed at him, gripping the control bar leading to the rudder, his eyes screwed against the force of the wind and spray, I again marvelled at his agility and enthusiasm. He was more like a school-boy than ever on that day, determined to try out his new boat.

Rounding the rocks guarding the entrance to the tiny natural harbour, we ran into waves that had now changed character. They had become long sweeping rollers, picking up our boat and bearing it along with a gentle gliding action that made us aware of the power of the sea. I had a sense of helplessness against the weight and force of the steel-grey water on which we rode so lightly.

The surface was covered with many thousands of black and white birds, floating in their huge flotillas as usual. Now when we were right among them, the sight became even more dramatic and impressive. As soon as the noise of the engine became too loud for them, whole battalions of the birds took flight, or at least attempted to fly. With the rush and force of their webbed feet making the water spray behind them, they ran with all possible speed over the long waves as they tried to gain momentum to rise. But they were all bad starters when it came to taking off quickly from the surface, and many dived instead as we drew right into the heart of the great flocks. Against the action of the sea, their natural home, they appeared beautifully equipped for the sharp dives that carried them quickly straight down into the deep water. After a few seconds they bobbed up again quite near to the boat, water rolling off their neat feathers, but if they were too close then they all dived again. The startled faces of the birds came very close to us: the neat dark beaks of the guillemots, the flattened faces of the razorbills, the curious and brightly coloured huge beaks of the puffins, all showed more clearly now than I had ever seen them.

We had shut the engine to a fraction of its power, and now glided through the massed birds, allowing the big swell to carry us along. Around us flew groups that were more curious than the rest. The razorbills and the guillemots had bodies that were cigar-shaped in their black and white compactness. They flew at speed, just above us. But the main groups scattered and flew far out to sea away from the small noisy intruder that had disturbed their fishing.

All along the base of the cliffs, against which the water was again breaking with sharp smacks and showers of white spray, deep cracks showed as small caves and grottoes. The rocks were smoothed by the action of centuries of waves washing over them as they jutted from the deep water beneath the cliffs. Here there is no shoreline; the ledges appear almost at water-level and are filled with long rows of guillemots, immaculate as these birds always display themselves, who regard us with curiosity.

The sea rushes into the grottoes, which echo with muffled booms as the waves reach into the farthest crack. Even in these grottoes, gloomy and cold as they appear, the kittiwakes have taken possession of every possible ledge.

With engine now silent, we allow the boat to swing with the waves into the entrance of one of the grottoes. Monrad has the oars out and handles the swaying boat with a skill acquired over many years of battling with the sea.

The guillemots do not leave their ledges close to the water until the boat almost touches them. Then with a concerted rush of black wings they fly as a compact group down to the water and swim away. The boat is carefully eased into the narrow opening, and at once we are released from the roar of the wind and the sea. The light becomes gloomy and the air very cold.

Directly overhead are the kittiwakes sitting in long lines on eggs now ready to hatch. The sunlight that still glows faintly, reaches down from the opening above us and makes their white wings seem transparent as they fly restlessly round the ledges. A constant splatter of excrement falls, and some of it strikes our jackets. The three of us are soon liberally smeared with a dirty mess, which we have to try to ignore. 'Kit-eee-wake'. . . the wailing calls are hugely magnified in this narrow and con-

fined space as the birds wheel and resettle, and then take wing
again.

The boat swings up and down with the rise and fall of the
waves as Monrad holds it as best he can against one of the jagged
rocks protruding from the water close to the darker wall. The
muffled boom of the water against the cliff face and the massed
cries of the birds all blend into a roar which makes conversation
almost impossible.

As we watch, groups of kittiwakes that had been to the pool
for bathing and then to the preening rocks, return to be greeted
individually with cries from their mates at the nests. Each time the
adult birds come together at the nest they make rapid head-
bowing actions to each other and give their heart-rending wailing
calls. Never do they seem to tire of the sound they make. Now, in
the last days of June, there were a great many eggs that had
hatched, and the nests contained some of the most attractive
youngsters of the cliffs, with their pale down and small black eyes
and beaks.

The sun was stronger now, striking sharply and directly on to
the side of the grotto favoured by the birds. The other wall,
slippery and cold as it was, obviously had no attraction for them.
Between the kittiwake ledges, sitting on eggs on ledges that contained no nests whatever, were groups of guillemots, including
the bridled variety, found in these northern waters, with a white
ring round each eye and a white streak running back towards the
back of the head.

The guillemots resented all the noise from their neighbours.
With heads that turned constantly to watch the movements around
them, they appeared to be ill at ease in such company. We wondered whether they would not have been happier away from the
squabbling of the kittiwakes. At times two of the white birds,
dove-like as they appear in flight, would engage in a furious fight,
interlocking their beaks and falling into the water with a flurry of
wings. It did not appear that the closeness of the nests made them
better neighbours, at least not as soon as the youngsters had

hatched. This was understandable for many of the nests touched each other and the adult birds hardly had room to turn round. Each seemed to resent the chicks of the other at such closeness, and pecking sessions started that resulted in the battles between the parents.

The big, handsome eggs of the guillemots had been adapted by nature for the comfortless and dangerous situation in which they were laid. Shaped rather like an old-fashioned spinning-top—one end sharply pointed and the other very wide—they could swing round and round on the ledges if the birds left in a sudden alarm flight, as they did at the sight of an eagle. Nevertheless, showers of eggs often fell from the ledges, lifted from them in a panic flight as they caught between the feet of the incubating birds, who stand in lines in much the same attitude as penguins over their eggs. With their bases of bluish-green colouring, boldly marked and blotched with dark brown or even black, they are indeed eggs of beauty. Larger and much more pear-shaped than those of the razorbills, they are very big compared to the size of the guillemot. They have thick hard shells as an added protection from the roughness of the ledges. Probably the fact that no two eggs really look alike in their markings helps the sitting birds to recognise their own when returning to incubate.

Above the confused noise, Monrad told me that he had gathered these eggs by the basket-full in his youth, often being lowered from the top of the great cliffs at the end of two ropes. He was light in weight and had the athletic agility of all the boys of the village, where climbing was as natural as walking. The eggs were prized for eating, being very rich, and many were preserved. The immature birds, returning to the cliffs for their first summer, were the trappers' main objective, and thousands were salted down for use in winter.

In places, especially along the Swedish coast, the trapping had been too intense, however, and in 1880 a small colony of some twenty guillemots was all that was left on the island of Stora Karlsö, off the east coast of Sweden. That year they were placed on the protected list, with the result that the numbers increased year by year, until now they nest again along the ledges of that white-walled island in their many thousands.

The guillemots very often form small groups as they had here between the kittiwakes, and even if their single egg is taken they return faithfully to the site that is their territory. If the egg is moved a little distance away, they will recognise it and try to drag it back again to where it was laid.

It is rather amazing that the chick manages to sustain life at all during the incubation, for the eggs often become thickly smeared with mud and excrement, making them almost impossible to recognise. But break through the thick shells they do, to emerge as pale small copies of their parents.

The black-backed gulls and ravens probably took more eggs along these cliffs than anything else, but the birds could replace the early losses by laying again some two weeks later. Monrad assured me that the egg collectors of the past had not reduced the number of nesting birds, as the many thousands of eggs taken from the ledges had been replaced in this way. But if the eggs were taken after this, then the summer nesting could be turned into a disaster.

It was impossible to converse more. It became too difficult to hear what the old man said above the booming of the sea and the shouting of the kittiwakes, a sound that echoed back and forth between the walls of the grotto in a hollow irritating volume of noise.

I wanted to land, to try to climb up the dark wall to a point where we could look directly into the nests on the sun-lit face opposite. Monrad was very doubtful, but he was ready to try. We held the boat against the rock face by using our fingers to grip whatever cracks were close to the boat. Ulla-Maija leaped with a sure-footed unafraid jump on to a narrow ledge, that was evil-smelling with excrement. She tested her foothold to find out how slippery it really was, and appeared satisfied. With some trouble I managed to hand her up the cameras, and then, with more luck than skill, contrived to sprawl on the shelf of rock myself, leaving Monrad alone to control the boat.

I cursed the birds at that moment as my jacket now had an odour from which I could not escape. It had to be endured for there was no way of cleaning ourselves here. Slowly and carefully we felt our way up the side of the cold wall. Each step had to be tested well. A false move and we should have been in the deep water below.

The upturned face of Monrad, with anxiety showing in his eyes, grew smaller as we mounted higher. We could not remain too long because he would find it too great a strain to control the boat alone in that narrow space between the walls. At last we reached a wider ledge on which we could place the camera on its tripod, and which gave us a wonderful, intimate view of the busy life opposite. The scene was lit in clear sunlight and could not have been better planned for our study.

The kittiwakes returned to the nests with food in a constant swirl of flashing wings. Most of the nests now contained two young, although there were still many sitting birds that had probably lost their early eggs. The guillemots were quite unafraid of us, refusing to leave their own eggs, safely and warmly held between their large dark feet. When one did move a little, bending down to look intently at its large egg in which it showed a considerable pride, it prodded it several times with the slim dark beak.

One or two of the birds did fly off, but without commotion or fear, and the eggs then rolled gently round and round to finally settle. They were left completely alone by the neighbouring bird, although it could easily have pecked at them. The sense of protection that the birds gave to each other in this way was obvious, and the gulls and ravens had little chance of taking these eggs so long as the remaining birds did not panic and fly.

When a sitting bird returned it first stood behind its single egg, looked at it critically for a while, then took a step forward and guided the egg carefully between its legs. Usually the large wide

G

end of the egg poked forward, to be glimpsed between the white feathering that covered and warmed it. Half-sitting most of the time, using a rock if possible for a support, the birds relaxed, closing their eyes for brief spells in the warmth of the sun. But their relaxation was continually disturbed by the kittiwakes, and a sense of restlessness was over all the ledges.

The ledges where the guillemots nested had a curious black-and-white effect because the incubating birds sat with their black backs towards the sea, whilst those without eggs faced us, eyes glittering in the sun and curiosity showing in the way they turned their heads from side to side to get the best view of us.

We knew that both the parents took turns at incubating and the hours must have dragged at times during the thirty-six days that passed before the youngster broke through. We saw two or three pairs change over, the sitting bird struggling upward from the egg as though it had cramp in its legs, whilst its mate watched anxiously until the egg was carefully transferred between its own feet. There was a little rubbing of beaks between the pair, then, thankful to be away out to sea, the bird released from duty swept outwards through the mouth of the grotto and landed on the swell.

A shout, reaching us thinly above all the other noise, made us look down at the small figure in the tossing boat. It was obviously time to descend, and as fast as we were able we slithered downwards, keeping as closely pressed against the wall as we could because of the sheer drop below us.

Without mishap, but not without a lot of misgivings about the jump between the rock and the swaying boat, we regained comparative safety by the side of old Monrad. He was obviously thankful we were down again. The controlling of the boat was sapping his strength, and it was with a grin of pleasure that he pushed the bows again into the bright light outside the grotto.

The wind caught at us with its usual fierce force. It needed the full strength of the motor to pull us away from the dangerous drag of the waves against the cliff.

Black shags sat in rows close to the water, holding out their dark wings to dry in the sun. As our boat came too close to them they rose in a black flock that resembled witches on their broomsticks. They have little charm, these shags, but they are as much a traditional part of the bird life of the cliffs as the kittiwakes. Their eggs were placed under protective stones or in cracks that were difficult to approach.

The swinging of the boat became more pronounced and the uneasy feeling in the stomach warned me that too much of this tossing would produce very unwelcome results! But Monrad seemed to have lost all thoughts of caution that morning.

We came so close to the shore rocks that the white tops threw back mists of spray over us. The old man handled the boat as if he was immensely enjoying himself and reliving old memories. His eyes twinkled and he was youthful with the joy of his mastery over the waves.

We cannot land anywhere, that is obvious.

'Let us take a fishing trip,' Monrad exclaims in the manner of a man who has wanted to do this all the time.

The boat pulls away from the cliff, into the more gentle rolling swell. When he considers the position suitable he cuts out the engine and holds the boat steady with the oars.

I am to try my hand at the long cod line. The immensely long thin nylon line, with its big lead weight and several cod hooks at the bottom, is lowered over the side. The water is very deep, and the line seems to snake out endlessly before it finally touches the bottom and the pull slackens.

I have to drag it up a couple of yards, then begin the long, rhythmic drawing up to the length of my arm and releasing again. It is the traditional method of catching cod, used for centuries by the small boats. Cod feed and swim very deep, and are attracted by the glitter of the baits moving up and down. There is a slight pull on the line: nothing big, for cod make no resistance at being drawn in, unlike the smaller coal fish, which give fight like small demons.

The last hook comes over the side and with it, held by Monrad reaching over and keeping it fast with a length of wood in which is embedded a long nail, a large cod. We all view it with satisfaction. The great shoals of winter have left the waters now and only a few remain around the rocks. Monrad gives a grin and spits out a mouthful of vile-looking chewing tobacco. He tells me to try again. We need the fish badly.

Now that fish have been sighted, the birds begin to gather around us. The motor is silent and we lie almost still in the water in order to fish for the cod. Several elegant guillemots appear, watching us closely. They seem to have none of the fear of the morning when the boat is silent. Over us assemble the gulls who sense fish from a great distance and follow every boat in to land in a big noisy flock. They are ready to instantly pounce down on every scrap thrown into the water as the fish are cleaned and the entrails tossed overboard.

Three more cod are soon taken, then follows a lengthy spell with no results of the line pulling. The light has become much worse. Grey clouds have obscured the sun that had shone so brightly on the wall of the grotto. The shudder of the boat in the waves is more pronounced, and I want to call it a day.

The sudden explosive burst of the engine causes instant panic among the birds that have gathered around the boat. Once more there is a great scramble and rush away from us, as some dive and others fly off in low groups almost touching the waves.

With a skill that is remarkable, Monrad carefully controls our course so that we miss the worst of the swell. Mostly we seem to be moving in the very depths of the waves that tower above us on either side, making any view of the horizon impossible until we rise again.

The sensation in the pit of the stomach becomes similar to that of being on a giant wheel. Huddling as low in the boat as possible against the coldness of the wind, I again look at Monrad to see how he regards our situation. Far from being concerned, the fight against the waves has stimulated him as perhaps nothing has done since he rowed with the open boats in the winters of the past.

At times even he is unable to prevent sheets of spray sweeping over us, and the cold sea water runs in rivulets down my face. Ulla-Maija is also showing signs of distress as she tries to protect her face, but the old man is quite unaware of our own troubles. He has time to point to where further long lines of guillemots stand regarding us with curiosity and wonder. It was frustrating to be so close to them and not able to land, but the seas gave them the protection they needed to be undisturbed in their summer life.

Rounding the last of the rocks shutting the village off from the sea, the quieter water is reached again. Thankfully I try to stretch out my legs and relax my hands which have been gripping the side of the boat so hard they have almost become glued into a set position. They show white and cold, and it takes time for the circulation to return.

The engine is again silenced and the boat glides to the end of the stone jetty. Here it was so peaceful that it was difficult to believe we had just gone through such rough and dangerous swells.

At the end of the jetty, faithfully keeping a watch until the boat returned, sat the two puffin hounds. They jumped up and licked the wrinkled face of Monrad as though they had not seen him for a very long time.

The fish is divided up between us as we sit in the dull light of the kitchen where a meal is being prepared for us. The warmth from the wood fire is welcome indeed and gradually the thawing-out produces a glow over the whole body.

On the table is a pile of newspapers brought over by a fishing boat. Each week the old man receives such a batch of reading, and in the evenings he carefully follows the local and world news.

On the front page of the *Lofotposten* a big bold black headline catches my eye: AT LEAST 700 GUILLEMOTS TRAPPED EVERY YEAR. The article is in Norwegian but is not difficult to read, and the subject matter one that we have so recently discussed.

Director Einar Brun of the Tromso museum had reported that he had now been out to Röst and seen for himself how the birds were trapped in the 'guillemot frames' which have been used for generations around the islands. At least 700 of the birds were killed in these frames at Röst each season, despite the fact that the trapping was now illegal.

Scientists wished to remain on friendly terms with the population and would try with all the means in their power to make the fishermen aware that the protected birds must not be taken for food.

'Is the population of guillemots and razorbills in real danger?' he had been asked.

'Yes. Thousands of the birds are killed each year by poisons, oil and also in salmon-lines. It was estimated that on and along the Greenland coastline a half-million birds are killed on the salmon-lines each season,' had been Einar Brun's grim statement. He continued with the view that the bird populations would not tolerate such a strain without reaching a crisis point.

I passed the article over to Monrad. He carefully read it as he puffed at his short blackened pipe which had stained his fingers through long years of use.

'When I was a boy there were many more birds than today,' he eventually grunted. 'People don't take the trouble here to collect the eggs today as we used to, even if the law still allowed it. Everyone has too high a standard of living now. But there will always be trapping for the guillemots and the puffins. You can taste why if you like!'

He rose and went to the larder, bringing back a big plate filled with the freshly cooked bodies of several puffins. The flesh was very dark and looked unappetising, but the taste was excellent. He rubbed the head of one of the two dogs who had brought down the puffins from the slopes. The situation over the past year or two had been bad, Monrad commented as we licked our fingers after the meal of puffins and potatoes. A great many of the young puffins had been found dead in the tunnels due to lack of food.

It was probably connected with the movement of the plankton, on which the crustaceans and the smaller fish were dependent, was my own comment. The broad lanes of travel usually carry these essential food supplies on a course suitable for the millions of nesting birds around Röst and Vaeroy. A slight change in the traditional movements, however, and the balance of the food supply is changed. Of the greatest importance to the diet of the birds, especially of the kittiwakes and guillemots, is the small herring-like capelin, which has a very wide range in the low Arctic waters.

Spawning in the west Atlantic, in an area ranging from Newfoundland almost up to Melville Bay, and in the east Atlantic from Iceland north to the cold depths of the Barents Sea, the capelin winter in very deep water. The early summer, however, finds them in countless millions in the shallow waters along the coast, in the big bays and along the deep fjords of the north.

Usually they emerge from the depths to fill the shallower waters with food at the time when the birds arrive for the summer nesting in May or even earlier. There the small fish remain, feeding themselves on the crustaceans with which these seas abound until about July.

When the capelin arrive near the coasts in May the males have a strange breeding attire that is not seen in any other fish. Two long bands of scales on either side of the body give them a very hairy appearance from which they have derived their latin name. Gathering in huge shoals, there is a big surplus of females as they near the coasts. These must seek places in the low clear water to deposit their fry. To a depth of three or four fathoms they sink to scatter the eggs, attaching them to the algae. So numerous are the eggs at this time that the water is stained yellow, and the eggs are visible in wide bands on the clear bottom. The males arrive and in big milky white clouds they discharge their sperm, so fertilising the eggs. This activity continues at the period when each day the light is longer and stronger.

The small capelins fall an easy victim to the many enemies that find them palatable: seals and Arctic char, cod and fjord cod as well as other fish make big inroads into their numbers, whilst to the kittiwakes and the other sea birds they are a source of food on which they depend all summer.

The ruby-eyed puffins possess an unfailing and little-understood instinct for being able to locate the underground lanes of small silver fish, mostly the young of the cod, that form their main diet. These broad lanes of flashing silver travel deep below the surface and do not remain constant in any one area. But the puffins know where to find them, even if they are a long distance from the nesting cliffs. Straight out to sea with no hesitation in their flight, the birds fly daily to where they know the fish will be found. Big webbed feet push the puffins swiftly down to the shadowy depths, where their strange beak construction enables them to catch and carry several fish. The thick tongue holds the caught fish firmly against the roof of the mouth while the beak can still be used to trap more. On the flight back, the fish are arranged in a neat row across their beaks, giving the puffins the appearance of having grown silver beards.

When the puffin young are hatched after some forty days of incubation, they are covered in long silky soft dark down, but the breast and stomach are white. The parents begin feeding them almost at once, and the first very small fish are soon replaced by

Page 113 (above) Elegant and fearless large white gannets; (below) in complete con-trast to the parent birds, newly hatched gannets are featherless and a dirty grey colour

Page 114   A charming young kittiwake

Page 115 Kittiwake with young about a month old

Page 116 (*above*) Big, untidy cormorants' nests of dried weed, perched on rocks covered in evil-smelling guano; (*below*) Ulla-Maija shares coffee with the old Norwegian fisherman Leif Eikset

larger rations. When the supplies of fish are limited for some reason, as happens during certain years along the northern coast, then the problem of feeding the youngsters can become acute. During the forty days that the parents bring back fish to the underground homes in the slopes, the rapidly growing, ever-hungry youngster can consume over two thousand small fish. This means a great deal of work for the parents and demands a huge food supply for the vast populations of the cliffs to be fed daily.

Not all puffins are nesting birds, of course, for they do not begin to take on the heavy duty of parents in the first years of their life. But with the big losses that are sustained each season, and the fact that only one egg is laid, the birds must have quite a long life span in order to produce at least two youngsters to replace them to continue the species at the present levels.

We were anxious to study the feeding puffins, but for the moment, whilst we waited for information about the location of a suitable eagle eyrie, we had to prepare for a further fishing-boat expedition.

9 *Northward Fly the Gannets*

Leif Eikset came from the same Viking stock as Monrad Mickelssen. Living on the northern seaboard of Vaeroy, where the winds blow in unchecked from the open sea, he has also known a great many Lofoten fishing winters in the open boats. Now he is the owner of a larger boat, whose engine has developed a protesting cough. He and the boat are growing old together, but the man and the creaking wood still have the will to face the swells in nearly all weathers.

With the good fortune that came all too seldom all summer, the end of June was calm enough to give us a good chance of visiting a small isolated islet of dark rock, smeared with a dirty white, that now gave summer quarters to an unusual colony.

For about three summers some eighty pairs of big white gannets had flown as far north as the islet off the slopes of Vaeroy, had alighted there and stayed to build what was obviously to be a permanent colony of their deep and strong dry seaweed nests. The oldest fishermen could not remember seeing them there before, and indeed to me they seemed to really belong to a warmer and more exotic climate than this unpredictable weather of the summer Lofotens.

From the coasts of Britain, Iceland, the Shetlands, St Kilda and the Faroe Isles to the islands round the Newfoundland coast and the Gulf of St Lawrence, the gannets, with their striking appearance and plunging dive-fishing methods, are to be seen in great or small colonies, but this northern colony was something quite new for Norway.

Leif Eikset seemed to have claimed the lonely little storm-swept island as his personal domain, for it was to him that we had to turn in order to visit these unusual visitors.

The water was calm, as it had to be for such a visit to have any landing chance, and Leif had also consulted the tide water carefully. A detour had to be made around the island of Mosken, rising with its massive slopes a short distance from the northern edge of Vaeroy. Sheep, appearing minute in size as they roamed in long lines along the almost non-existent paths at the very summits of the great peaks, were the only inhabitants.

Eikset, face tanned reddish-brown with years of weathering, a mass of wrinkles round his eyes due to the force of the winds, pointed to the grass that rose high and very green up the sheer sides of the grey mountains. This had always been cut for the hay that was so essential to the islanders for the feeding of the sheep in winter. It seemed impossible that a human could possibly secure a foothold to cut grass from such slopes, and indeed the work had to be done by the cutters being lowered at the end of ropes from the summit.

The scything was far from easy, but had never been neglected. As the grass was cut so it fell to the rocks below, to be gathered by the women and youngsters into bales, loaded into small boats and transported back to Vaeroy. There it was hung in long lines to dry in the wind and sun. The grass was extremely rich in quality as winter feed, and as the sheep were able to roam free and unchecked from spring to late autumn on the slopes, finding their own living, it was little wonder that the owning of a flock of sheep, however small, was the natural order of life for the fishing families.

The haze of heat made the islands in the distance shimmer and dance. We were now in an area of water that had excited the imagination of writers of the past, including such masters as Edgar Allan Poe and Jules Verne. Here ran the famed—and often feared by the open boats—Moskenes Current. This immensely powerful tidal bore, through which a vicious surge of grey-green sea sweeps daily with the incoming high tide, made Eikset turn the bows of his vessel away from the island of the gannets so that we could make a big sweeping circle to avoid the tide-race. But even from a long distance we could see the big white forms, the black tips to the long wings showing clearly, as the gannets flew over their nesting rocks.

The old boat was cleverly steered so that we could begin to ease slowly towards the island. Many small rocks projected from the water or were just under the surface, and these had to be avoided, requiring all the concentration of which the old stout man in the soiled blue jersey was capable. From his high cabin he peered out of the open window, and when he had come as close as he dared, the engine was shut off and the anchor lowered.

It was something of a thrill to now be so close to the gannets who had come so far north for the sake of the rich fishing to be had in the waters around the tidal-race. The rocks were not high, and were so covered with a dirty excrement that it would have been impossible for the gannets alone to have been responsible. Much older colonists of the island were probably the chief cause of all the mess, the smell from which soon made itself known to us even from a distance over the water. As we neared the islet a big black cloud of cormorants had risen, circled once and then steered in a high-flying group towards another island some little distance away.

These had been the rightful owners of the islet for many years, and they must have resented the intrusion of the gannets into their domain. They had none of the courage and devotion to their nests and eggs or young when disturbed that the gannets showed so plainly, but we knew that they would return as soon as our boat left the area.

We rowed to the low rocks, over which we could make a rather precarious way to the solid land. In the warm sun the stench of the guano, covering the rocks and the spaces between all the nests in a greenish evil-looking mess, was almost over-powering.

Eikset remained in his boat, engine now just ticking over, watching the tide closely. The tide controls landings such as these as much as the calmness of the sea, and it is not often that the two factors are ideal. We had not much time in which to study the life of these mixed birds of the sea at the end of June, when they now mostly had young in the close massed deep nests.

Almost touching each other it appeared at first, the gannets did not move from their nests at our approach. There was enough space between each nest, however, for the birds to be out of striking range of each other, but any bird landing in the space between several nests was immediately pecked by the vicious strong and pointed spear-like beaks of the sitting birds.

The pale cream necks and heads, the sharply marked lines around the pale blue eyes, and the general immaculate whiteness of the large and heavy bodies gave an impressive appearance to the colony. The birds regarded us with curiosity, eyes never leaving our movements, big beaks ready to snap into action.

In the deep nests, which seemed like islands in the midst of the awful guano into which our feet sank at every move, were many newly hatched single youngsters. They were as ugly, with their dark blue-grey rough skin covered with a shimmer of pale down, as the adults were splendidly regal.

It would be several moults before they would attain the pure white bodies of maturity. Of immature youngsters there was no sign on this island. All were mature nesting birds, and the young were probably having summer in a warmer climate than these northern seas. All winter the gannets that nest around the English coast had probably enjoyed the sun of Spain, Portugal or the coast of north-west Africa, but gannets are essentially birds of the sea and their behaviour away from their nesting rocks is not so well known.

They have a dislike for land which is easily understood when one sees how clumsy they are when attempting to rise. A good uplift from a strong wind is necessary, and in this respect at any rate, plus the lure of the good fishing, the gannets had chosen well for a northern outpost.

They had arrived at this islet early in spring, long before the eggs were laid, and Eikset had watched them fishing as a group. Their plunging concerted diving into the heart of a shoal of coal fish we were also able to witness, and the memory of it remains strong. With wings held close to the cigar-shaped bodies, streamlined for just such a purpose, the large white birds would suddenly drop into the water with long beaks pointed downwards like spears. The blow they received on the breast as they struck the water was lessened by the shock-absorbers that are formed by air-sacs under the skin.

They did not spear their prey, but gained enough depth from their plunging dives to follow the shoal until they could seize and swallow the coal fish under the water. One after another the birds rose to the surface, where they floated high, the water rolling easily in large drops from their very efficient water-resistant feathers.

The new-born young are blind and helpless at first, and it is a wonder that they are not suffocated or crushed by the weight of their heavy parent. During the long period of incubation the old bird had sat with one large dark foot over the single egg and the other placed over this. This had given sufficient warmth to hatch the egg after some forty days or so, and when the adults warmed the young they continued with the same procedure as with the egg. Why the youngsters were not crushed is a tribute to their powers of survival!

Very soon the youngsters that were so naked in the first nests we viewed would be covered with an attractive thick white down, and those that were about ten days of age had now begun to take their food direct from the throats of the old birds. They had an instinctive desire to keep the interior of the nests clean and squirted their excrement over the edge of the nests, which was the reason for the build-up of the evil-smelling mess all around us.

When the young reached the age of about a month and a half, the gannets flying back and forth with their feeding fish would lose interest in them and feeding would become very irregular, ceasing altogether in another month. For several days after this the youngsters would have to live on the fat they had accumulated during the intensive feeding, and when the hunger pangs became too great, the young gannets would leave the safety of their deep nests and make for the edges of the rocks.

The young sit and try their wings in the wind for a time, and the parents now ignore them completely, although they are still sailing around their island outpost far from land. If the wind is right when the young try first to fly then they can sail upwards and feel the power of their wings. But if they attempt to fly on a calm day, then they usually end up by bumping down the rocks until they eventually reach the sea below. They immediately begin to swim away from their birthplace, making for the south. When their supply of fat is exhausted, they are light enough in weight to be able to at last rise and fly, and towards the warmer lands of the south they set their course in winter flight.

The gannet colony on this lonely island between the southern tip of the Lofoten chain and Vaeroy occupied the highest rocks, and the sprawling colony of cormorants was spread among the lower slopes.

There they had a great many wide and deep nests of dried sea-weeds, and the hatching had been very successful, judging by the number of young in many stages of growth occupying all the nests. Of the old birds not one remained, but the greater black-backed gulls, who flew round us all the while we were there, had not been given the chance to take either eggs or young. Even out here they were hopefully patrolling, but both the gannets and the cormorants had protected their nests well.

The newly hatched young cormorants were a match for the gannets in ugliness, being born naked and very dark with long necks and grotesque over-large heads. Those a little larger had acquired a rather clownish charm, however. Attired in a fluffy blackish down, they sat on the edges of their nests with huge dark webbed feet splayed out to keep their balance. In the heat of the morning their cheek pouches flapped wildly. After about a month these youngsters would be full-grown, and would soon learn to become efficient divers pursuing their prey along the bottom of the shallow sounds that are so plentiful in the north. The smaller fish they would catch would be swallowed whole when the birds came to the surface, but those that were too large would be thrown into the air, to be recaught and then swallowed. This is probably to ensure that the fish is stunned sufficiently to be less troublesome as it is sucked down the long throat.

But the cormorants and the shags, diving birds as they are, have feathering that is not really suitable for their way of life. The water soon becomes absorbed into the feathers if the birds remain too long at their diving, and it is for this reason that long rows of the birds are so often seen with outstretched wings, allowing the wind and the sun to dry them.

Some of the nests that lay fixed firmly to the flatter parts of the small island were very large. They had been used before and had been added to with fresh material this summer. Year after year the cormorants had nested on the island, for there they were undisturbed and had been the main occupants of the rocky island until the arrival of the gannets. Now the birds were uneasy neighbours, tolerating each other but keeping strictly to their own kind.

The gannets, from their higher more closely-knit colony, appeared much too well-bred and immaculate for the dark cormorants. There was food in plenty for both the species around their isolated island home, however, and the birds would probably remain in possession of the rocks for many generations to come if they were unmolested.

We were reluctant to leave the island, although the stench was now making a sickness of the stomach that would not be helped by any rough seas! Fortunately the water had remained calm. Soon all our equipment was back on the fishing boat, much to the satisfaction of Leif Eikset who had been anxiously watching the tide water rising and gurgling between the rocks.

As the boat drew away from the island, which slowly receded into the blue haze, we watched the gannets diving for food amidst a shoal of fish some distance away from their nesting rocks. The cormorants rose in a black cloud as we neared the other island on which they were perching. In a long line and flying high, they at once returned to settle over and around the nests containing their young. On days of storm force winds and rain, the island must have been covered with spray from the waves, especially on the lower shelves where the cormorants had their big nests. But judging by the large number of youngsters the birds did not suffer from the weather nor from the attentions of black-backed gulls who winged over them. In late summer the big dark birds would fly southwards for the winter, and the rocks would be cold and deserted until the following spring.

The anchor was dropped close to the cliffs of Mosken. Leif Eikset appeared anxious that we share the lunch he had with him. From boulder to boulder we jumped to land amid the small round stones at the edge of the water. The boat was left unattended, swinging gently as it pulled at the anchor chain.

From a large seaman's bag the old man produced loaves of home-baked bread, butter, and two glass jars. From the first jar came what we thought was a fine pink salmon, and tasted as such. It was, however, coal fish, prepared to an old northern recipe. The old man sliced the bread into thick slabs and invited us to try the false-salmon together with the reddish-brown mixture of

H

rhubarb and ginger that came from the second jar. We sat in the
welcome and unusual warmth of the sun, washing the food down
with big cups of steaming coffee. At that moment, in the great
silent calmness over the water, there was a feeling of peace that
was rare indeed.

Over us winged a sea eagle. It brought my mind back sharply
and unpleasantly to the problem that remained unsolved. Where
were we to find these great birds nesting in a position that allowed
us to study their life?

I turned to Eikset for help as we watched the eagle sailing and
circling high over us, on the watch for an ailing bird. It saw a
kittiwake that was struggling alone on a rock where no birds
usually came. The bird was sick, and the eagle swooped down and
picked it up in one great claw. Rising upwards it was gone again,
to disappear over the peaks behind us.

Eikset paused for a time in his eating, playing with his old knife
as if deep in thought. He studied us carefully as though he had
not before been aware of our presence. Rubbing an unshaven chin
he looked at the sky. We wondered whether he was going to
discuss it at all.

'Umm . . . we shall see,' was the eventual outcome of his thinking, and with that we had to be content.

I would have asked again, but Ulla-Maija silenced me with a
look. She had become friendly with Eikset on the trip, and the
old fisherman suddenly gathered up the remains of the bread and
the two glass jars with their delicious northern mixtures, and
handed them all to her with a broad grin on his lined face. He
had noticed how she had enjoyed his food.

We thanked him profusely. Our own rations were always very
scanty.

Conversation was limited on the way back to Vaeroy. For once
we could travel over the water in some degree of comfort. We
sat on old upturned fish boxes and watched the intense glitter of
the sun on the calm sea. Many thoughts kept us quiet.

My own were concentrated on the sea eagles.

When we left Leif Eikset after docking quietly at his small jetty, I had the feeling that he was thinking over my question as to the whereabouts of the eagles . . . At any rate I could hope so.

Later that evening we had a visitor to our rorbu. The young man came in quietly and sat gazing down into the water outside for a time. Then he announced in a shy way that it had been arranged that we should visit a lonely island where he lived in the heart of a great archipelago off the mainland. His fisherman father and he knew where a pair of eagles were nesting on a small islet that was never disturbed. He had contacted his father and they were willing to show us the eyrie if we kept the whereabouts and name of the island to ourselves.

We looked at him as though we could not believe what he was saying. Recovering after my own immense surprise and pleasure, I asked him many questions, and when he eventually left we slipped into our sleeping-bags hardly daring to hope that we were at last to have a close look at the birds we had come so far to see in the intimacy of their home life.

10 *Lonely Island of the Sea Eagles*

The constant necessity to travel by boat whenever a new area had to be explored made for heavy work in transporting our equipment and supplies. Gathered around us were a profusion of packages as we waited for the steamer to carry us back to the mainland on the first stage of our expedition to the island of the sea eagles.

My fervent wish at that moment was that we could have the power to travel as lightly as the birds above us.

The date was 1 July and still unusually warm and calm of sea. The wide Vestfjord channel that separates the mainland from the Lofoten chain and Vaeroy sparkled in the sun. The contrast was very great between its present mood and the biting cold fury into which the sea could be whipped in the winter storms of the long dark days and nights.

Our own stay on the mainland could be counted in hours. We had again to reload everything on another and much smaller vessel. Named after one of the host of small islands lying a few miles offshore, the small steamer was one of the life-lines connecting the scattered islands to the mainland. Summer and winter, in waters that remain unfrozen due to the influence of the Gulf Stream, these boats know very little rest.

The islanders depend greatly upon them, and it is very rarely that they arrive late at the little jetties, loaded with post, supplies of every kind and a few passengers. On the darkest and stormiest of winter nights, when the storm lanterns dance at the end of the piers, the steamers arrive. The hour is never too late for them to be met by a small crowd, for they remain a magnet that brings out both young and old to the waterfronts.

In the soft glow of a remarkable summer evening with its unexpected calm, we glided between the mass of islands forming the wide spreading archipelago. The wash from our sides brushed gently against the rocks of island after island, rising in low humped-backed masses from the still water.

It was to one of these, slightly larger and occupied by a few families who had long known their life of isolation, that we were being carried.

We had given the family the promise they needed that we should not divulge the name of the island. At first they had been reluctant to even invite us over, and only after the son had managed to talk the family round to his way of thinking were we considered a suitable couple to be shown the silent eyrie far from human disturbance. We had known Sven, the son, for some time on Vaeroy. He had kept quiet before about his knowledge, but a word from Leif Eikset had been enough to send him to our rorbu with his invitation.

Each pair of the birds that nested around the Lofotens and Vaeroy was carefully protected, in utter contrast to the days such a few years ago when the hand of every man seemed to be turned against the eagles in their struggle to survive.

Gently the bows of our craft swished through the quiet green

water until we reached the small pier on which we were to dis-
embark. Gazing at the group on the pier as they loomed ever
larger, we wondered whether we should be met. Four cheerful
smiling and tanned faces beamed down at us and the men helped
to carry our equipment from the boat. In single file, all of us
carrying packages on our shoulders, we trudged along the narrow
pathway leading away from the pier towards the few scattered
wooden houses forming the hamlet.

The variety and the wild beauty of the plant life along the sides
of the sandy road and the banks rising around us made me stop
in admiration and soon I was a long way behind the others. It
was the richest collection of plants and clovers I had seen in the
north. My companions understood little of my enthusiasm. I was
commenting on something so usual to them as to be unseen by
their eyes.

Our tent was erected in the heart of a field thick with purple
and white clovers. Everywhere in the grass were big clumps of
yellow, mauve, white and blue flower heads that had us stepping
very carefully to avoid crushing them. Close to our camp was the
sea, lapping quietly against the low shore rocks over which a
colony of Arctic terns flew and screeched. The sea was a pale
transparent green of great beauty, with every rock reflected
deeply in its mirror-like surface.

We were invited to the family house. Over coffee and sandwiches we discussed the eagles.

The hour was now very late, approaching midnight, but we
were not to be allowed much rest that night. The enthusiasm of
Sven and his younger brother of about fifteen was such that they
had arranged with their father to take out his fishing boat even at
that hour and show us where the eagles nested. We were as
eager as they were to see them in the low and soft light that
flooded over the water and threw every rock into a black relief.

As we left our small harbour the air was mild and caressing
to the face. The engine sound was greatly magnified in the other-

wise immense silence that lay over the water. The sun showed as a huge orange globe just above the horizon.

All around us and stretching into the dim distance were small islands. They glided slowly past as we chugged through a sea turned a deep orange by the low sun. No scene could have had a greater beauty or more quiet drama than that first July night on the way to the islet of the eagles.

The island loomed darkly closer, rising higher than the others around it. Beneath the dark grey walls of the nesting cliff our fishing boat drifted quietly, with engine silenced. The channel between the eagle island and another small lower islet, on which we were later to have our camp, was very narrow and the boat had to be carefully steered by the younger son, who showed himself to be remarkably proficient despite his youthful years.

The anchor was quietly dropped in mid-channel. Sven gripped my arm and pointed upwards.

Soundlessly, swinging from a high point on the top of the second islet, came the huge dark form of one of the eagles, alarmed at our approach and wanting to take a closer look at us. The gloom between the cliffs was deep where we lay in shadow.

Greatly magnified in the dusky air of midnight, the eagle sank even lower until it hung almost motionless in the manner of a kestrel above our heads. The wide wings scarcely moved. It was slightly uncanny to gaze up and watch this silent hovering bird, wing-end feathers expanding outwards like the outstretched fingers of a hand, watching our every move.

Sven again pointed upwards along the cliff face. Straining my eyes and blinking to see better in the gloom, I found it possible after a while to locate the ledge on which were the eaglets. It was very hard to distinguish it from any other ledge in that poor light, however. The grey rock of the cliff face was covered with lichens in various shades of grey and black. Against such a background the brown feathered now completely still forms of the two youngsters were an invisible part of the landscape. There was no huge pile of building material to form a prominent nest: merely a ledge at one end of which a small rowan ash tree stood quiet in the windless night.

For some minutes we remained at anchor, whilst the eagle remained a lonely, huge silent sentinel figure above us. It made no sound either with wing beats or voice.

The uncanny silence, now broken by the distant muffled call of a gull or tern, made the scene all the more impressive and dramatic. Through me pulsed the exultant thrill of having at last come so close to the birds at their eyrie.

The anchor was pulled up slowly and without undue sound, and we drew away from the channel with engine at half-throttle. Skilfully steered by the younger son, the fishing boat ploughed easily through the sea, now slightly lighter as the sun began its upward rise again.

The very early dawn was already too light for any easy sleep for me, but the tent was welcome for a few hours of relaxation. The day had been extremely long and we had seen much to tire our senses. The haunting sight of the eagle, dark and silent as a huge shadow over our heads would not leave my vision, even with closed eyes.

The following morning was as calm as the previous day. How long this fine weather could continue we did not know, but we were in the centre of a high-pressure belt and were thankful for it.

In the bright light of mid-morning the fishing boat again quietly chugged towards the eagle island. The drama of the night was dispelled slightly by the brightness of the day, but the sense of excitement was there stronger than ever.

We hoped to build a shelter of natural materials on the island, from which to study the eagles at close range. Our only regret was that we had not discovered this site much earlier, for now the young were so large that the parents would give them little attention during the day. Feeding would probably be very early in the morning and in the evening.

Viewed in daylight, the island proved to be an ideal site, not only for the eagles but for our studies. There was no heart-breaking sheer cliff to be climbed here, with the ever-present danger of a fall to disaster. The island rose to a high central plateau, from which we could look down on to the eyrie ledge. From below, we could also have a good view of the nesting site from one of the boulder-strewn grassy mounds close to the sea.

It took me only a fairly short time to climb up to within so close a range of the ledge that the eaglets appeared very large. The nest had been flattened by the birds until it had lost all shape. The rowan ash tree managed to provide a little shelter from the sun which hit at the cliff face for most hours of the day, causing the eaglets to pant with discomfort, their beaks wide open.

For some time I gazed at the birds, who returned my stare with cold unblinking dark eyes. Silent as two brown-feathered statues, they regarded me inquisitively. One was a little larger and bolder than its companion, as is usually the case with sea eagle young, which are born with an interval of several days between them.

Already the birds had an air of dignity in their upright and frozen stiffness, which they had assumed on seeing us below them. Their huge claws gripped the edge of the ledge, and only the occasional blinking of the eyes showed that they were alive.

From their own level I could gaze out over the sea as they did and view the world over which they would soon fly. The sun had risen to a mid-morning height and warmth, and the sky was unclouded. A million points of flashing light sparkled from the water, dazzling my eyes so that it was not possible to look down for more than a second.

Into the far distance the islets grew small and bluer. They appeared to float as if suspended between the earth and the sky, for it was difficult to see where the water surface began. The resemblance to floating pale logs drifting slowly along a giant river was very marked where the islands showed through the heat haze. Composed of very white rock in places, their low slopes were adorned with green vegetation, splashed with mauve, white and bright yellow flowers. In the farthest distance the line of mainland mountains showed as a pale blue wall.

From afar came the muffled cries of common gulls and from near at hand the cloth-tearing screech of the Arctic terns, who were nesting in a colony on the long finger of low rock jutting into the shallow water at the end of the islet on the farther side of the narrow channel. This islet came in for my close inspection through the binoculars. It should make an ideal base for our camp. The eagles would certainly never tolerate strangers camping on their own island, but they might accept us on the farther lower flatter island. Its highest point seemed to serve as a favourite perching site for the eagles, who then had a wide and uninterrupted view over the sea in all directions.

Through the glasses I could distinguish the bright red of the ripening cloudberries, and the sight was enough to heighten my enthusiasm for a small island that was completely isolated.

The shallow water between the two islands had an almost pure white bottom composed of countless millions of finely ground shells. Against this, and clearly visible in the pale green clear water, a forest of dark brown seaweeds lazily swayed back and forth with the movement of the tide, which was high at that time.

In the centre the channel was much deeper, and here the fishing boat could anchor safely. We had come ashore in a small rowing boat, keeping all movements as quiet as possible for we had no wish to disturb the peace of this silent world over which the eagles had ruled for many years.

On the rocky edge of the eagle isle a thin wooden jetty, its long piles almost rotted through, poked out into the still water. In the long and unkempt grasses close around it, the ruins of what had been a neat small wooden house were all that remained to show where a young couple from the mainland had tried to build up a life in this wilderness. From this height I could clearly see, in sharp outline in the hard light of the sun, the grey skeleton of the house, the beams and the broken boards weathered a pale silver-grey by the years.

My companions were gathered in a small group around a black-tarred rotting boat that lay keel upwards close to the tiny natural harbour once used by the young fisherman who had built the house. Many years ago, when the big open boats with their square brown sails and central masts had set out in their flotillas from the Nordland villages, making for the great cod fishing grounds of the Lofoten islands, the timber for this lonely outpost had been transported with much effort to the island.

Like so many other Norwegians, the young newly married pair had the strong desire to live far from others in a world where they were free and masters of their own fate. Around them they had the black guillemots for companions all summer, and the terns and gulls. The eagles had not then taken possession of the nesting ledge.

One early summer the island had known human life, and for a short while all had gone well. But there is no certainty in life either for bird or man, and the death of the young wife in child-birth had been the killer of the dream. The house, with the possessions so carefully gathered around it, had been abandoned to its fate. The winds and winter gales had torn with their relentless northern fury at the shells that were left of the dream. Without mercy the lonely home had been battered, the creaking boards broken loose from the stout beams. But the name the couple had given to their island remained . . . Home Island.

Sven related this story to me after I had clambered down the cliff to where the group were lifting the old boat in preparation for bearing it up to a patch of grass and rocks from which we could obtain an excellent view of the eyrie. We would place the upturned boat on rocks, leaving enough height under it to enable us to sit upright, and then surround the boat with boards and vegetation. With luck this would not disturb the eagles, although they would be certain to note at once that the boat had been moved to a strange place. By using only the materials that were at hand and to which they were accustomed, we had a good hope that the old boat would make a very useful hide from which we could film through a slit in an old tarpaulin.

As the others worked to prepare the hide, I left them for a while to wander among the ruins. Coldly depressive even on such a brilliant day of sunshine were the symbols of a way of life that had once been and was no more. A thin whistle of wind passed between the broken boards of what had been the living-room wall facing the sea. An old clock lay on the window sill, its face covered with small glass fragments.

Sodden with many rains but still wearing the grotesque smile that had been stitched on its face, a rag doll stared up at the ceiling from the littered floor. The two buttons forming the eyes were still in place, giving the doll the appearance of life even after many years. From an open drawer of an old cupboard fluttered the remnants of several garments. I picked up an account book, in which the cost of various food items had been written in a childish but neat hand.

Rotting ropes and tackle, made with much care and patience, lay on the floor of an outside shed which smelled heavy with mould. On a ledge, under one or two roofing boards still nailed to the beams, ravens had built two strongly constructed nests. Skeletons of several small birds were mixed with the seaweed and sticks. A forlorn sadness about the whole scene began to affect me greatly and the calls of my companions were a return to welcome reality.

We completed the hide, making it as natural as possible, and as we admired our work from a short distance away one of the eagles returned from an expedition over the sea. Seeing the group far below, it flew in a wide circle round its island, silent as ever. Then it retired to settle on the highest point of the islet on which we planned to camp. This was obviously a well-liked vantage point, and from there we were to watch the eagle for many days. There it could also watch us, and would gradually grow accustomed to our quiet movements.

Even from a long distance the old female appeared huge and majestic. In colouring she was almost white on the head and breast, a white mixed with brown to give a rather dirty effect, the usual sign of a bird that is very well matured in years. It was certainly the largest eagle I had seen and as it watched us from its high perch, sitting very upright, there was about it an impressive air of being the ruler of this world.

Looking at it there, feathers ruffled in the light breeze, my thoughts returned to the young couple who had once started their married life here with such hopes. Home Island . . . even the name had been full of promise. But now only the eagles remained. To this pair it was indeed Home Island, and had been now for some years. They were growing old as the ruins beneath them rotted more visibly each season of their nesting.

Midnight: the fishing boat gently glided to a stop in the centre of the channel. This time we were to be put ashore on the rocks and remain in the hide for the rest of the night. The tide was very low, exposing the thick brown and very slippery weeds that clung with great strength to every rock covered at high water. They made our progress dangerous and slow.

Making as little sound as possible, we climbed up to where the upturned old boat was fixed between the rocks under the eyrie. We crept into the confined darkness and the vegetation was carefully replaced around the boat sides.

Our small cramped prison reeked strongly of tar and of the sea. We could not leave it again until the boat returned in the middle of the following morning to take us off. Every movement had to be carefully thought out for there was little space to stretch out. The camera had to be placed on a very low tripod and a survey made of our sight through a slit in the old dark grey canvas that had been thrown over the boat in a natural manner.

The hardness and sharp angles of the rocks did not encourage comfort, but the sleeping-bags we had under us eased the situation quite a lot. The bag containing our precious thermos flasks, filled with boiling water for tea, was pushed into a crack with care. We should certainly need the drink before the long vigil was over.

We could just discern the nesting ledge in the poor light. Although the midnight sun was illuminating the sea with a rosy glow, our cliff face was in darkness until a little later in the early morning. From the eaglets came no movement whatever, and the only sound to break the great silence was the receding noise of the fishing-boat engine.

The overpowering odour of tar and old materials, heightened by the cramped space in which we half lay, affected our senses so that it became almost impossible to remain clearly awake. We had to take turns in watching the cliff face, for we had no idea when the old bird might return with food to the ledge.

Gradually the sun swung round and the light grew stronger minute by minute. At three in the early dawn, during one of my spells of watching, the first pink flush of the sun caressed the summit of the nesting site. The utter silence that had lain over the island all night was broken now by the thin wheezing calls of the black guillemots, themselves very early risers.

The orange-yellow light bathed more of the cliff with its early glow. It reached the ledge on which the eaglets squatted. It was the sign for them to awake. With much shaking of the brown feathers the two birds rose and stretched themselves on the very edge of the ledge. They surveyed the world below them with sharp dark brown eyes, over which the pale grey inner eye lids moved frequently.

From our hide, which was completely ignored by the eaglets, we could observe them very well. There was now none of the stiff rigidity that had held them when they had seen us close to their eyrie on our first visit. They appeared immense already in the dawn light, and feeling they had their domain to themselves they began the morning exercises that were an essential part of their growing up.

Coming to the edge of the ledge, the larger of the two commenced a long series of trial leaps into the air with wide wings flapping with all the force and speed it could manage. It was watched by the other youngster, who remained seated at one end of the ledge to give room for the other to continue its morning training.

For a second or two the big claws left the ledge and the bird was held in the air. But the strain was as yet too great and it sank back, to sit for a time panting with open beak even in the coldness of the early morning. The slightly younger bird then rose and began a rather half-hearted imitation of the wing flapping, after which both birds began to push each other along the ledge, wings held open, in a fighting display only intended to strengthen their muscles.

Soon tiring of this, they sat motionless on the ledge edge, gripping the rock with their over-large claws, whilst they gazed out over the calm water with every sign of impatience in the small head movements they made from time to time.

From above them came repeated distractions. Crows and gulls flew over, gave shouts of annoyance or alarm as they beheld the two silent forms, or paused in flight at the sight of food remains on the ledge.

A greater black-backed gull and a hooded crow, more daring than the rest, settled close to the ledge. Obviously they were trying to find enough courage to bring them to within thieving distance of the fish remains. But although they came very close, the lure of the fish could not overcome their fear of the eagles, and they left.

We found the strain of watching the cliff face without pause very great. The grey and black lichens blended into the general colouring of the rock, giving it such a camouflaged effect that it was immensely difficult to concentrate the gaze for a long time on one spot, especially as we had had no sleep at all.

We did not want to miss the coming of the parent with food. We knew she could swing along the face and drop it on the ledge and be away again in a matter of seconds. And so far we had not heard a sound from the two eaglets.

To combat the boredom of waiting, the youngsters began a long and very careful preening of their feathers. This occupied their total attention for the next two hours, during which the light grew ever stronger on the cliff face, and the air inside our hide became stiflingly hot and stuffy. Each feather, especially those of the tail and wing tips, was pulled with care between the slightly opened beaks. The youngsters showed great patience with this toilet, and when at last they felt it was complete, their appearance was quite immaculate.

One of the birds went to the back of the ledge and brought back in one claw the remains of a large coal fish. It tore at this breakfast food, watched by the other eagle, who made no move whatever towards trying to get a share until the larger bird ceased eating. Only then did the younger bird tear at the food.

The wind had risen slightly and they stood with feathers ruffled in the breeze, keeping a fixed gaze out to sea.

We were feeling the strain of the night and the watching, and our nerves had become tight as we looked at our watches and saw that it was still very early. Hot tea from the flasks and a pile of sandwiches helped to keep up our spirits, but we were longing to stretch our aching legs after having them curled most uncomfortably under us.

Had the eagle come to the ledge without our seeing it? We could not be certain, but the action of the eaglets showed that they were still waiting, so we had to keep the eyrie in constant sight.

Our field of vision from the hide was small, but I managed to clear away some of the vegetation from the rear to give me a glimpse of the world from that angle. As I made my first report back to my companion, trying at the same time to breathe in some fresh air, the huge and welcome form of the eagle came into my sight, high up and flying directly towards the cliff.

With bated breath, for we did not know whether she would

accept the hide, we peered through our observation slit. The eagle circled the island twice, came lower over the hide and decided it was not dangerous. She then swung along the rock face without a sound and landed just as silently on the ledge with wings held high. At once the two youngsters crowded on both sides of her, their own wings waving.

She dropped a large fish, that had been held in one claw, and without any further attention to the eaglets rose again and was gone. The whole action had not taken more than a second or two, and not a sound had been made by either the parent or the youngsters. The larger of the two now began to tear with great eagerness at the fresh fish, his big beak already capable of rending any prey to pieces.

We could breathe out again after the long vigil. I had tried to record on film the return of the eagle and we could only hope for the best. The soft sound of the camera had not worried her in the least, and we had the satisfaction of knowing we could observe the birds from this hide without disturbing their life in any way.

The confined space in the hide grew even hotter. The watch face now read ten in the morning. We listened with an anxious intensity for the faint chugging of the fishing-boat engine. At last, growing louder with an infuriating slowness, the sound reached us from far over the water.

Voices below were the welcome evidence that at last the boat had arrived. A rowing boat scraped against the rocks, and seconds later a face peered in at us from the rear of the hide. The eagle was not in sight, and quickly we scrambled out through a small gap. We stood in the clear fresh air, breathing deeply whilst the circulation slowly returned to our legs. After our long confinement the air was like wine in our lungs.

We climbed thankfully aboard the boat and a warm sun beat down upon us. As we steamed away from the island, the ledge growing ever fainter, the old eagle returned, to follow the boat for a distance. Seeing that we meant her no harm she returned to

I

settle on the topmost point of the islet we were soon to make our lonely domain.

The islands lay on the glassy water, every rock faithfully reflected so that it was almost impossible to know which was the reality and which the reflection. At that moment it was easy to forget that conditions like these were exceptional, and the mood could so quickly change. We could not rely on such ideal conditions for a camping expedition to the islet opposite the eagle èyrie . . . we could only hope and prepare for the winds and rain to which we had become so accustomed.

11 *Life in Dramatic Isolation*

It was time for the cutting of the hay. The scythes were out all day and long into the evening. Every patch of grass and clover, however small, was precious for winter feeding. None was too small to be missed, or too difficult to reach.

On long lines of thin wire the sweet-smelling grass is hung to dry. In the calmness of midnight the men are still working. With sudden restless anxiety a pair of brown-winged birds with long down-curving bills fly in circles around the cutters.

They are curlews, who until that time had been rather silent and little seen in their movements. Now their musical alarm trills echoed with unexpected wild music over us as we tried to sleep. The light was very bright and to those who like darkness for the night, sleep comes in only restless fits at this period of eternal light.

The fishermen had a good idea where the three young, well camouflaged in their down of speckled brown, had hidden in the long grasses at the first sign of the cutting coming too close to their territory. They would try to avoid the area but the curlews were not to know this, and winged with the fear of parents who would risk anything to draw attention away from the young.

I lay in my sleeping-bag and listened to these sounds of the wild. My thoughts were of the eagle pair and the two young which they were so successfully rearing. The desire to pack and make for the isle opposite their site was so strong that in the early dawn we were up and making breakfast. There is something about the dawn in this northern world that affects the mind and the body. The beauty and the silence is so intense that one longs to capture and hold it so that it can become a permanent part of life. But it cannot be and so one lives it to the full on the calm mornings that are so rare.

A light mist appeared as a thin haze over the water, quickly spread and covered the face of the sun so that it showed as a cold white ball. A slight rain began to fall. We looked at each other with a sigh of resignation. Was this the end of the fine spell? It was very probable, for it had already been of unusual length and warmth. Summers in these northern waters certainly are not hot, and we had grown accustomed to wearing many warm clothes.

Our equipment was again packed when the mist and rain cleared for a while, and in the early afternoon we loaded it all on to the deck of the fishing boat, together with a milk churn for a water supply. There would be no fresh water on our isle and we must hope that we should not be stranded for too many days without a visit from the boat. But we could not rely on this; everything would depend on the weather.

From mid-channel we rowed ashore, making several trips to deposit everything on the low rocks by the water's edge. The anchor was drawn up and the boat pulled away. We watched it grow smaller, then looked round at our small domain, feeling a sense of isolation in this silent world of the low islands.

From our position we could clearly see the nesting ledge over the channel. Of the eagle there was no sign for the moment, but over us screeched the Arctic terns that nested on a long finger of low rocks at one end of the isle.

We searched for a suitable place for the tent on the low and rather swampy land with its springy thick vegetation that grew between every rock. We found a spot that looked directly over to the eagle eyrie, and when we had erected the tent, dragging our possessions to the site with some effort, we gazed at the eagle that had now returned and was circling over us.

It came lower, looking now immense. The wide white tail was fanned out so that the sun that had returned in a rather watery ball made the feathers appear almost transparent. The half-open beak was a dull yellow, and we could clearly see the dark eyes that followed our every footstep as the bird came to a halt in flight over us and began to hover. It had no fear of us as far as we could see, but for the whole time we were camping close to its eyrie it kept us under a careful survey. We were trespassing on its territory, and although it made no protesting alarm cries, it showed by its hovering above us and the low circling sweeps it made round our camp that it would follow our every move.

The female was the guardian of the territory. Of the slighter smaller and darker brown male there was little sign. He did return later that same evening and the two birds flew together, wing tips almost touching as they rose higher and higher in the clear air over the cliff site. But he was soon winging out to sea again, leaving the female to resume her place on her vantage point, which was now behind our tent on the highest point of rock. There she could keep a close observation on us, but she had no intention of letting our closeness disturb her habits.

We were thankful she seemed to be accepting us in this way. In the evening light we explored this wild plant paradise into which we had strayed. Our feet sank into the deep spongy undergrowth from which the ripening cloudberries glowed in splashes of bright red. Soon we could have their golden sweet richness for a dessert. Between the rocks were the flowers of this nature garden glowing in patches of white, yellow, mauve and pale blues. In the dim distance the mainland mountains rose as a misty blue.

We gathered driftwood and soon the thin grey column of smoke from our first campfire rose straight into the still air, for as yet there was no wind. Over the hot flames we cooked our evening meal, eating it in the great stillness from which there was no escape. There was no desire to talk. We had reached our goal and were in surroundings of such beauty that the desire was strong at that moment to remain forever in such an island paradise.

The night was very quiet, the sea tinged with the glow of the midnight sun. As the light increased in the early dawn I studied the ledge opposite our tent through my binoculars. The eaglets had begun their morning exercises.

Under them and close to the sea, a large pile of rounded boulders had formed a solid mass that was the home of a colony of black guillemots. The only sound that reached me in the dawn quietness was their wheezing. At regular intervals pairs of these chubby black and white little auks returned from their fishing expeditions. Flying very low on swift-beating wings they either made wide swinging turns that brought them finally on to the rocks above the water, or landed with a splash and a shower of spray on the still surface close to the boulders.

From high over them the eaglets gazed down, watching with curiosity. The guillemots formed small groups on the water, swimming close together and gossiping in their thin high voices. Most of them still had two eggs hidden in the dark recesses under the boulders. There were many that had young, however, and at frequent intervals the parents would return with the long red eel-like fish that seemed to form their main diet in the north. These they held quite delicately in their thin dark beaks as they first swam with them in front of the nesting rocks. Time after time they would dip head and fish under the water, and when this ceremony was over, then a swift flight and a rush into the nesting hole was the procedure.

The desire for a fire and hot tea drew me very early from the tent. I had no idea whether the eagle had returned with morning food for the young, but from this distance I could see her when she flew back. Our position was ideal. Soon the blackened old kettle had boiling water sizzling into the red glow of the fire. Life felt good on that early morning of continuing calm and beauty.

Our small rowing boat was stranded high among the rocks, where the high water had left it. The difference between high and low water here was about six feet, and we had much difficulty in dragging the boat between the rocks down to the water level at low tide. There were no landing places except by crossing the very slippery weed-covered rocks.

We rowed in the direction of the long finger forming the eastern end of our island. Here nested both common and Arctic terns and the ultra-delicate white and grey birds were soon weaving around our heads as graceful as ballet-dancers. There were still many eggs left in the scrapes of nests between the flowers and the grasses that covered the rocks, but the greater black-backed gulls had already claimed a large share of the eggs and young of the colonies.

The screeching swallow-like birds with their black skull caps were not afraid to face their black-winged foes when the gulls invaded the air over their territory. The deep baying 'auk, auk' of the slow-flying black-backs was a constant reminder to the terns that they would never escape from the unwelcome attentions of their main enemy in this region.

As we watched from our drifting boat the whole colony of Arctic terns nearest to the water's edge rose in a concerted attack directed against a pair of black-backs that had dived towards eggs left unattended for some moments. The gulls twisted and turned and shouted in deep-voiced annoyance as they were chased off. They did not go far, however, merely flying to the highest point above the colony, where they could watch for the moment when their attacks would be more successful.

The terns were very restless incubators. Sitting still on their eggs seemed to bore them immensely and they would rise again after a few minutes, to weave above the nest in a screeching flight before fluttering down to display the slim white wings high over the black caps. Among the multi-coloured wild plants they made a perfect picture of white-grey charm.

When the colony slept was unknown to me for almost from the hour of midnight, when the sun again began to rise into the heaven from its lowest point close to the horizon, their brilliant wax-red feet and beaks would be above us. They belonged entirely to a world of sunlight and eager movement, diving to catch their small silver fish with small plops in the quiet sea.

It was almost impossible to think that soon these seemingly weightless birds, who looked as if they would be swept off course by the passing winds, would set off on a long-distance migration flight unequalled by any other bird. In the latter part of August the terns would concentrate on feeding well in order to build up a thick layer of fat. In the high Arctic regions they would depart before the end of August, whilst in the lower zone the last of the birds would leave in September. In small parties of between ten and twenty they would commence the long flight, during which they would neither feed nor rest. On their slim, sharp-angled wings they would maintain a steady easterly or south-easterly course, keeping about 100ft above the sea.

Page 149   The sea eagle, lord of the skies over Mostad, no longer trapped as in former years

Page 150 (*above*) Sea eagle young at about seven weeks old; (*below*) this young eagle, larger and more active than its companion, spent hours preening its brown feathering

Page 151 Young sea eagles on the eyrie, still silent but powerful, with a hard

Page 152 (*above*) The lonely island where the gannets and cormorants share their summer nesting; (*below*) the light of the midnight sun shining over a rare evening of calm on Home Island

They would probably remain in European waters for a short time to regain their strength and to feed, but before the end of October they would all have left Europe to continue flying southwards along the west coast of Africa, keeping well out to sea. Some of the birds remain along the African coast all winter, enjoying a rich diet, but the majority sweep onwards to the waters around South Africa. At times they round the Cape, going north again into the Indian Ocean where they are seen as far as Madagascar. Large numbers of the terns journey even farther south, crossing the 'roaring forties and shrieking fifties', braving whatever storms the seas throw against them, until finally they reach the waters of Antarctica. There they winter, making for clearings in the ice-pack belt, feeding on krill which is still very plentiful.

In crossing the globe almost from pole to pole, the Arctic terns complete a winged journey that is longer than anything undertaken by any other animal or bird. During their time in the Antarctic they can again bask in the continuous light of the midnight sun, and in this manner the terns live in more sunlight than any other living thing. But to achieve this the birds that seem so frail have to undertake an amazing migration of at least 13,000 miles twice a year.

How many of the young that were hatched on our own small island would ever reach maturity it was hard to say. It did not appear that the gulls would leave many alive long enough to ever fly off in their long flight in search of the sun.

Rain fell in the evening and the air grew cold and damp. The tent was welcome and we listened to the steady but quite soft patter of the drops on the canvas and hoped that it would not develop into a storm.

In the situation we were in there was no desire to stay in the sleeping-bag longer than necessary. I am as restless as the terns and at first dawn I have the need to be out to watch for the eagles. The sky promised a fine day after the light rain. Soon the scene became dramatically beautiful as the wind rose and the deep grey

and white billowing cloud formations mingled to fill the heaven
with a wild grandeur. The long grasses and the many flowers
shook violently in the wind, and as I stood facing the force of its
clean whine, the female of the eagles returned to swing along the
cliff face. Then she rose and hung almost motionless right above
the eyrie for a time, looking down at the youngsters, a large fish
dripping water held in one claw.

Dropping suddenly with both claws held straight downwards,
she alighted on the ledge, released the fish and was then away
again, being borne upwards by the wind. She made hardly a move
with her wings, allowing the currents of air to lift her effortlessly
upwards. Then she settled on the highest rock above the eyrie
and allowed the wind to ruffle her feathers as though she was
enjoying the return of an old friend.

When the gulls and terns saw her they rose as a body, and several
made whistling diving attacks that stopped just short of the upturned head with the vicious beak. The eagle ignored these, but
we were to notice that she was never allowed to perch in peace.
The eagle attracted the anger and attacks of all passing birds in a
similar manner to an owl found in a tree in daylight. Crows,
ravens, gulls and terns all found her a target for their wrath and
diving flights, and when she grew too tired of their persistent
attentions she would rise from her favourite rock and head out to
sea. Even on this flight she was pursued and it must have been in
sheer relief that she eventually rose higher and higher until she
became a speck in the heaven.

More rain came sweeping in over the sea which was now grey.
Mist brought down the visibility so much that we could not see
over the channel. But the cloudberries were now ripe enough to
gather, and around the evening fire we could enjoy their delicious
taste, together with fried fish and the home-baked bread that we
had brought out with us.

Suddenly in the night the storm winds broke over us. We
had dreaded this, for there was no other shelter except for our

tent, which now seemed terribly fragile. The canvas shook so fiercely that all thoughts of sleep had to be abandoned and we watched with anxious eyes as the walls blew in like the sails of a ship in full flight before the wind. Slapping and shaking as though the canvas would tear itself to pieces at any moment, the tent nevertheless held firm, much to our utter relief. We covered everything as best we could and hastily dressed although it was barely one in the morning.

But suddenly, with the dramatic swiftness that is so characteristic of the north, the storm passed over, the wind died and the rain ceased. The sun returned as a watery ball and the island steamed around us.

In this very early damp dawn we made our hot tea. We always gave good thought to the wood for the morning fire, keeping it dry so that we were always sure of a swift blaze. It was necessary.

The midnight sun dispelled the gloom of the storm sky, and soon it was again touching the eagle eyrie on which the youngsters had sat huddled together during the storm. The rain had run from the feathers they so carefully preened and oiled, and as the sun reached them they rose and shook themselves vigorously. Immediately they began their morning preening; then exactly at 3.30, with the sun growing stronger on the rock face, the broad wings of the female swung in from the sea. A fish held firmly in her claws, she landed for the briefest of seconds on the ledge. Then she was gone again.

As the sun grew stronger so the mist and steam rose in thin hazy clouds from all points of the island. The effect was of an almost unreal scene, with our own sense of isolation heightened by it all.

Exactly two hours after the first feeding the female made a second trip to the ledge, again with a large coal-fish in her claws. This time she stopped for a short while with the two young who seemed really pleased to have her company. They crowded round her, glad to have her large and dependable form close to them even for a brief spell. They had been well provided for each day of their growth, and at first the food had been torn into small portions for them to swallow. But, with their increased growth and strength, they themselves had been expected to pull into strips the fish and birds that formed their diet. They had no teaching to know how to do this, and had either learned from watching the parents on the ledge, or found out by trial and accident how they must tramp on the prey with their claws whilst using the beak to tear it apart.

After feeding, the eaglets commenced their practice jumps. With a frenzy of energy the wide wings that seemed too large for the birds were worked up and down, and with a push from the outstretched claws they were able to remain off the ledge for a few seconds. It was plain that they were longing to be in the air. Each time the gulls passed over them they turned their heads to follow their flight. The ledge would not hold them captive for much longer and soon they would know the sheer thrill of rising into the wind and soaring upwards into the high clear air over their watery world.

As the sun again became a rising ball of heat, lighting every drop of rain water that still hung from the leaves and petals of the many plants with a rainbow of colours, the female returned to settle quietly above the eyrie almost on the top of the cliff. Still as she sat, she was almost invisible, blending so well into the mottled background of the rock face. She remained in regal isolation, the breeze ruffling the near-white feathering of her head and neck. She turned and gazed out at sea many times as though expecting her mate to return, and when at last the brown wings of the male did appear from the direction of the open sea, she rose to meet him.

Together they circled the eyrie site, wing tips almost touching, wings held motionless as the air currents carried them in sweeping circular movements round our camp site. Suddenly and unexpectedly, a series of sharp high yelps came from the birds, who began to roll over and over high above of us though they were enjoying every moment of this morning.

Home Island . . . the name came to me again as I watched them at their effortless play. We were witnessing a sight that was becoming more rare each year . . . the undisturbed flight of a pair of eagles over an eyrie that contained two healthy and rapidly growing young. The thrill of it all affected my own senses so that I wanted to hold its memory in my brain forever.

For the first six years of her life, the female flying above us had winged summer and winter over the islands of North Norway, waiting for the time when she could assume the white tail of maturity. When she felt it was time for her to seek a mate, she had begun to search for a suitable nesting ledge along many cliffs and over many islands. At last she had found a young male as yet unmated and together they had tumbled on their broad wings in play high above the sea.

Their deep and instinctive fear of man made them search for an eyrie site as far away from the haunts of humans as possible. In the heart of the great archipelago that was so little inhabited, they had seen on a cold February morning the deserted house, the rotting sheds, and a ledge on a cliff face that seemed ideal for their first nest. Circling round the tiny island many times, they at last sank down to examine the ledge at close range, had alighted on it and decided that it would suit them.

For longer than the oldest fisherman in the small village from which we had made the boat trip could remember, the ledge had been used as the place for an eagle eyrie. When the young eagle pair saw it in the growing light of a new year it was deserted. The pair that had been its owners were no more. The female had died and the lonely male had left the island to wander southwards.

So the first sticks had been gathered to start new life again on the ledge. The old nests had been flattened by generations of youngsters and blown away in the winter storms. The young pair did not construct a very large nest of sticks, being content with the flat ledge with its protective wall on three sides and its tiny rowan ash tree in one corner.

But sheep wool had lined the nest, for when the first eggs were laid the weather was still bitterly cold and they would need all the warmth they could obtain. The young and now mature eagle had sat day after day, unable to leave the eggs because of the cold, whilst her mate had returned to the ledge with fish.

For some forty days she had faced the winds and the rain, looking down on a world that the pair were to know for many years. The first eggs had hatched and the two young had broken through, covered with greyish-yellow down.

The female was always the chief provider of the food the family needed. The diet had been mainly of coal-fish or sea birds. She was not a very expert hunter and never grew to be, and the sheep that wandered over the slopes with their lambs in spring knew they had little to fear from the eagles as long as their families kept together. Only when a lamb sickened and died did the eagle wing down and carry it off in her strong claws.

June and July had passed with the eaglets growing each day larger and stronger. Their down had been replaced after some three weeks by a denser brown feathering and soon they were eagerly trying their wide wings in their anxiety to be away. But for ten weeks they had remained on the ledge, trapped until the day they at last lifted into the air in first flight.

High into billowing white clouds they had used the wind as the parents did to bear them effortlessly upwards. By this time they had learned to use their voices, imitating the parents in their high-pitched yelping cries of 'kri-kri-kri-kri'. But they were never very vocal birds and only uttered their cries when they were alarmed or in bursts of occasional pleasure in their flying together as a family in the late summer.

The four had spiralled upwards until they became black specks in the blueness of the August sky. But the young had to learn to hunt for themselves and at first they had been clumsy in the extreme. Failure was the usual result of their dives. The fish usually eluded them easily and only the birds that had dropped in death on the rocks were taken.

Patience and the ability to try again and again had to be slowly instilled into the eaglets. The sight of one of them was enough to cause panic among the sea birds that still remained around the islands, and for a time the eaglets were glad to return to their nesting ledge, where they could sit in peace for hour after hour.

The old birds taught them well, however, and they learned the value of being able to sit silent and still for hours on a rock above the water, waiting for the right second to pounce on the steel-grey back of a fish passing unsuspectingly beneath.

Probably their proudest moment of the late summer had been when they pulled from the sea the struggling form of their first fish. Crushing this in their powerful claws they would have taken it back to their favourite perching rock, to be devoured with a pleasure they had never known before. No fish dropped to them on the eyrie ledge would have been torn to pieces with such proud energy.

But the time for soaring as a family could not last. By the dark days, when the snow and the winter winds had returned and the Home Island lay bleak and desolate, the family had separated. The youngsters had left their island to wander southwards, and if they survived their first winter they would have to fly for several years as immature young, waiting for the year of maturity when their own nesting life could begin.

The old birds had continued to sweep the skies around the islands all winter. The fishermen knew them well, and the birds would drop down quite close to the boats in their hunger, losing their fear and knowing that fish were to be found where the men were working. The long cold frozen months caused them to take risks they would never do when food was more plentiful.

But the winter had passed and they had survived, to return again to the nesting ledge on Home Island. The pattern had been repeated, and for some years now the same birds that we were watching had occupied the ledge from the early months of the year until the early autumn. They would remain in a faithful marriage for the whole of their years over the island until the day came when one of them would fail to return from a hunting trip. Its body might never be discovered, but the survivor of the pair would remain, sitting gazing out to sea expecting to see the brown wings return at any time. Some old birds never left the sites they had shared with a mate for years. Silent and alone they winged until death also claimed them.

I was aroused from my deep thoughts by a call from my companion. Two young wheatears shouted lustily close to our camp as they tried to keep contact with the busy female who picked insects from the rocks and vegetation at great speed. It was a time of the summer when growth must now proceed with speed. The young of all the species must be prepared in their body structure for the rigours of autumn and winter. Fat must be stored for use when the time for lone hunting came.

A pair of wagtails fed their four young, pale copies of the adults and all furiously bobbing their long tails among the water rocks. An eider with three young swam slowly by the camp, closely escorted by three spinsters who had appointed themselves unofficial guardians.

Over the water close to where the black guillemots had their colony a line of dark shags sat with outstretched wings. The scene was peaceful indeed until a high piping, similar in tone to that of the oystercatchers, made me look more closely across the channel.

I glimpsed the brown form of a sea otter moving from hole to hole, searching for eggs or young of the black guillemots. His shrill calls were to frighten the birds from their nesting holes. Soon the air was filled with the thin anxious wheezing of the black and white birds as they left in a flurry of wings. The otter reached the water, dived in without a splash and swam behind a rock mass to be seen no more.

Brown butterflies hovered around the heads of the sweet-scented valerian in greater numbers than I would ever have thought possible on the island. The fierce glitter of the sun on the sea was so blinding that it made one feel that the rest of the world was probably only a mirage and that this tiny isolated island was the only reality.

Days of close contact with the eagles and their way of life had deeply affected our own thinking. If it had been possible we would have wished to stay and be accepted as a part of the nature with which we now lived on such intimate terms.

K

12　*The Long Flight*

It is now the middle of July and the rain has returned, sweeping dismally over our small island. The water runs in rivulets down the sides of the tent, filling every pot and pan that we can place out to catch it. We are in bad need of water for we have not seen the fishing boat that should have come to take us off from our isolated site.

The eagle comes with food at 6.30 in the evening, as we crouch over our small fire in the open. Shortly after we hear the chugging of the engine of the fishing boat, and watch it with much pleasure as it drops anchor in mid-channel. We can have fish and some fresh water, but we decline the men's offer to take us from our island. We have no wish to leave, and the sons promise to return again when the weather makes it impossible for us to remain. We have decided to chance the erratic whims of the northern summer days and nights and hope that the storms are only of short duration.

We have had very little sleep indeed during our period of

isolation. Never in our sleeping-bags before eleven at night, and out of them by two in the morning had been the regular routine, and now when the dawn comes with a dull deep grey gloom it feels difficult to awaken. After several such nights one feels that it is impossible to continue without a long rest, but the desire to watch for the eagle at her feeding in the very early mornings is so strong that it overcomes all other emotions.

Several mornings we have had the rowing boat out into the channel by just after two in the morning, making for the decaying shed on the piles that once formed the small jetty on the island of the eagles. This has made an ideal place from which to study them, much better than the upturned and cramped boat. In this shed, filled with a mass of old ropes, broken boxes and round flat red weights for the nets, we have spent many draught-filled hours as the wind whined between the cracks.

From here we have been able to observe the ledge more closely and see the immense size of the returning eagle as she comes to the ledge in the early light with food. Several times the prey has been a kittiwake, a puffin or even an eider, as well as fish.

The eaglets have at last found their voices! It has taken them a long time for up to now they have always been silent in all their actions. But suddenly, on a morning when the mist makes us shiver violently and long for the warmth of the sun, they give yelps of anger as ravens pass too close above the eyrie.

The ravens are flying as a family of seven, for a pair have nested on the farther side of the cliff and have been as successful as usual in launching a large family of black youngsters into the summer world. They seem to have a desire to fly each morning close to the eaglets, croaking with their deep baying calls. But the eaglets do not waste their replies. Eagles seem to have no desire to call to the same extent as most other birds.

From a long distance we could see the big female returning from her hunting, being mobbed and insulted as she passed first over a colony of common gulls and then over the region of the terns.

Each group took up the chase over their own areas, and hooded crows and ravens also added their quota to the noise that followed the eagle. The sounds did not subside until she reached our island, but even there the ravens were ready to make life noisily unpleasant. It was little wonder that she preferred a lonely rock out at sea for most of the day hours.

The cloudberries were now large with golden ripeness and in certain areas the blueberries were also at their best. Eaten together, these berries made a delicious combination. It is strange how human tastes vary. To us the blueberries have the most mouthwatering taste, and the black crowberries are bitter and very unappealing. The Eskimoes, however, pick the crowberries with pleasure, but even the birds will not usually touch them, and it is difficult to understand what is their attraction. But over the northern world the berries grow in their countless millions to give a welcome addition to the diet.

Where all was flashing life over the finger of rocks among which the Arctic terns had their eggs, there has now settled a tragic silence, only broken by the deep 'auk, auk' of the black-backed gulls who resent my presence under them. They appear to have cleared the site of every egg and youngster. One feels a bitter anger towards the big robbers, whose appearance of beak and eye is one of cruelty.

With the departure of the terns some of the beauty has left the rocks. The flowers seem wilted and forlorn and robbed of their vivid life. The remaining terns have retreated to another strip of low rock farther away, over which they now fly with angry shouts. It is not easy to see how they manage to rear their young here each summer for they are never free from enemies.

As I stand and curse the black-backs, the female eagle wings above me coming down to a low height. She seems to have become so used to me that her fear has left her. But she arouses the wrath of the black-backs who rise with deep calls of alarm. With slow beats of her wide wings, carrying her at a very good speed, she continues on her course out to sea. It would have pleased me better if she had turned and ripped at the black-backs with her huge beak, but she ignored them.

I returned to the camp rather sorrowfully . . . there was no respite from the old laws of nature even in this lonely world of small islands.

By the early morning the tent was shaking in another very fierce gale. We had become tired of the wetness, for it was becoming almost impossible to keep our equipment dry.

We faced the thought of another wet morning with little enthusiasm and wondered what we should do. We had no means of communicating with our friends at the fishing hamlet.

At six in the morning, with a grey mist falling after the dropping of the wind, we heard the engine of the fishing boat. Our friends had considered it was time we should leave the island. The weather forecast was very bad, and they feared for us if we were caught in full storm conditions.

Thankfully we packed and loaded everything on to the deck of the boat, but there was a real reluctance to take farewell of the camp site and the eagle island. It was with a pang of sorrow that I watched the two islands growing ever smaller as we plunged through the choppy water.

Whether we should see them again we did not know, but the eagle had seen our leaving and followed the boat for some way, circling high above us. At last she turned and flew straight back to the island on which we had camped, settling on her perch on the tallest peak of rock. She was visible until the islands disappeared from our sight in the mist.

The old school-house is glimpsed again through the rain as we reach Mostad in the very late evening after a rough journey over from Vaeroy. We are tired and wet, and thankfully light a fire in our small room. The day seems to have consisted of a week, and we realise we have been on the move for some twenty hours.

The storms break with full fury and we are glad that we left
our small island. There is no respite from the wind and the rain,
and for several days we are confined to the school-house. The
cliff birds have an unsheltered life, especially the young of the
guillemots who are exposed to all this bad weather. They have not
the protection that the puffins and the razorbills and the young
black guillemots have from their nesting holes.

As July draws to a close the weather improves, but the wetness
in the ground persists. The sun again warms us, however, and
dries the cliff face down which rivulets of water pour from the long
soaking.

The eagles of Mostad have been successful with their breeding,
flying now over the cliffs as a family of four. The eaglets appear
much smaller, brown of tail, and lack the skill of flight of their
parents, but they will learn more each day. The cliffs facing the
open sea, where the kittiwakes have their greatest number of nests,
make a good training ground for the eaglets. One of the adult
eagles patrols along the sheer face of the great cliff that rises from
the sea, watched by the two young who sit passive and intently
concentrated on what is happening along the ledges.

The kittiwakes now have a great number of youngsters of about
a month old. They perch either on the edges of the nests or sit
precariously on the narrow ledges from which at times first one
and then another slide off into the choppy seas that constantly
dash against the grey rock. Many of the young are lost in this way,
for they are picked up by black-backed gulls or swooped upon by
the eagles. Even the eaglets begin to try hunting flights over kittiwake fledglings that have fallen from the ledges. This infuriates
the whole mass of kittiwakes, who must be on their guard now
against the raven family, the gulls and the eagles. It is not surprising
that their wailing cries never cease. Their only protection is in their
numbers.

Young kittiwakes have a far greater charm at this age than the
scrawny and unattractive young of the various gulls. They have
very deep blue-black intelligent eyes, a black nape of neck band,

pale grey wings with a black band and even black at the tip of the white tail.

We rescue two of the small birds that have fallen from the ledges and take them back to the school-house. Food for them comes from the many shell-fish clinging stubbornly to the rocks exposed at low tide. The fish are snapped up with an intense eagerness, but one has to be very careful of the sharp dark beaks. They can dig into the finger like a needle, drawing blood. We soon found it necessary to shape the hand to resemble the open beak of the adult bird, for the young kittiwakes obtain their food by pushing beak and head deep into the throat of the parent.

There was little fear shown by the two we had saved. Very quickly they found a ledge at the corner of the school-house where they would remain quietly for hours until they were fed. There seemed to be no desire whatever on their part to attempt to fly. Eventually I decided to see whether they could use their wings. Tossing one of the pair high in the air I watched anxiously to see how it would react. There was no need for fear, however. The wings opened and with a light buoyant soaring flight the small bird flew round and round the school-house. Tiring of this, it then headed out over the water and along the shoreline, landing on a big boulder by the water. Sadly I thought it was the last we should see of this youngster, but within an hour it was back, sitting beside its companion at the corner of the house on its flat ledge of rock.

The two we had adopted had not the slightest intention of leaving. When the school-house door was opened they walked into our room, poking their slim beaks into all they could reach. Each time we threw them into the air they merely flew the length of the deserted village, to return to their ledge where they waited to be fed. We could only hope that when the urge to migrate came to the masses on the cliffs, these two would also take flight out to sea.

For the moment we had to feed them. As we searched for the shell-fish on the wet shore rocks they followed us, but had no liking whatever for water. They scrambled quickly out if we placed them in the shallow pools between the rocks.

Back at the school-house they would sit for long periods carefully cleaning their young feathering until they were very neat and tidy. The instinct to preen seems to be one of the strongest of all emotions in young birds, as we have found by the study of so many.

We grew fond of the young kittiwakes, but they belong to the wide and open seas. In August the whole kittiwake population of so many thousands of birds would suddenly take flight and disappear out to sea. During September and October they would move leisurely southwards, keeping to the coastal waters and then spreading out into the deep oceans. They are quite independent of land, feeding on small crustaceans, fish fry and minute game in the upper layers of the water. They have no need or ability to dive deeply for fish as do the auks.

At the end of October and into November the majority of the birds would be arriving at their winter quarters extending over the wide expanse of sea in the southern parts of the Arctic and the northern regions of the boreal area. The delicate-appearing kittiwakes are especially attracted by the cold currents and fly with ease over the Atlantic. Even in midwinter there would be mass flights of the birds over the gales of the North Atlantic and groups from many of the bird rocks mix together in enormous flocks.

Birds that had nested in America would cross the Atlantic to the east and fly along the western European waters, but the majority of the long flights are westwards towards America. Out in the deep oceans the kittiwakes often follow the big liners and cargo ships, and, apart from the fulmars, they are the birds most often seen in the central seas of the North Atlantic.

But it is the youngsters who are the greatest travellers and we wondered how far our two kittiwakes would wander before returning to the rocks at Vaeroy. They would not begin to breed until they were two years old, so there was good time for them to try their powers of long flight. They would probably fly to the cold currents of the West Atlantic to find a rich supply of food, and possibly along West Greenland's coastal waters. Here they might well fall victim to the massed killings that have always been a part of the winter life in this area where the kittiwake flesh is greatly prized for food.

If our two youngsters survived, they would continue to roam over great distances until they were ready to breed; then they would return to the Vaeroy cliffs from the ledges of which they had slipped into the sea. The instinct that brings them winging back to the very same ledges on which they were hatched is little understood. The birds possess some inherent sensory powers of which we know nothing.

But although the young kittiwakes might travel immense distances until they felt the urge to mate, they would eventually return to make circling flights around the old school-house. We wondered whether we should be there to greet them.

13 *Hard Days in the Grim Grotto*

The great concentration of puffins and the other auks, plus many thousands of kittiwakes, is centred around the part of the sheer cliffs close to Mostad known as Bryningsholm.

Unless the tide and weather are very favourable it is impossible to make a landing. The ideal conditions occur very seldom indeed, and the birds have an undisturbed life as far as human intrusion is concerned. The litter of small caves, ledges that come right down to sea level, and jagged rocks that push out of the waves to make perching places for whole armies of the birds, all form one of the most impressive sights on Vaeroy.

At the rear of these sea-edge crevices and grottoes rise high and dangerous slopes, covered with grass and earth for much of their height. This is the summer home for literally millions of puffins. Until one has actually seen them in this one area, gathered around their nesting tunnels, it is impossible to imagine the impression made by their sheer fantastic size of population.

For many days we had waited, anxiously watching the sea for signs of returning calm weather. Our good Norwegian friend, Ronald Johanssen, was to attempt at the first opportunity a landing among these millions of birds. We should travel with him, taking our camping equipment and a supply of water in plastic containers.

Old Monrad was very dubious about us going at all. He knew the water and the cliffs so well, and had grave doubts as to whether we could manage alone. But it had to be done if we were to really get to know the birds intimately before it was too late in the season.

The sun was watery but the sea fairly smooth on the morning we saw the small boat crossing the bay and heading for our small stone jetty. The engine could be heard clearly from a long distance and we recognised it. One soon learns to distinguish one boat from another by the voice of its engine.

Ronald had a boat of about the same size as that owned by Monrad: open to the weather, wide of beam and driven by a powerful if small outboard motor.

We loaded up, cursing the long trek through the sheep droppings to the jetty. With so many packs and pieces of equipment, travelling by open boat in the salt-water spray presented a problem each time we made a move to another island or part of the cliffs. When we started, the boat was low in the water with the weight it carried. A swell was running that had not been noticeable from the shallow harbour, and soon we were rounding the arm of the cliff that protected the village from the worst of the seas.

When the almost vertical cliff face rose above us, and the boat rose and fell rather frighteningly in the swell around the rocks, I wondered whether it would be possible for us to make a landing anywhere. It seemed very improbable.

Examining each yard of the cliff face, we were watched by the massed battalions of immature guillemots and puffins gathered near the edge of the water on the low ledges and favourite perches. From many of the ledges that had some sort of overhead protection, dark shags looked down at us with suspicion and alarm. From their deep nests of dried weeds the long-necked youngsters stretched over the sides to watch us as we swayed very close to them.

A narrow-mouthed grotto, its sides covered with green slime and the nests of a great many kittiwakes, was to prove the best probability as a landing site. Even here it would take all the skill and strength of Ronald and the young fisherman he had brought along to help him, if we were to get ashore without accident.

He let the boat surge with the tide into the grotto. At the rear loomed up a dark wall, through which a ragged hole had been torn by some accident of nature when the cliffs were first exposed to the light. Through this the wind shrieked. Through it we could also see to the great high slopes that were our objective.

The grotto looked as uninviting as any place I had seen since we landed first at Vaeroy in early May. Every slippery rock at the base of its slimy walls was covered thickly with the excrement of many birds. There was an overpowering stench of decay, and the dull booming of the sea and the roar of the wind through the hole in the cliff face did not help to brighten our first impressions of what was to be our camping place.

It needed as much luck as courage and skill to safely negotiate the almost non-existent ledge along which we had to crawl to reach the rocks at the rear of the grotto right under the hole. The wall was too slippery to give us handholds and to transport all our packs along this path needed combined team work that took time and tremendous physical effort. Without Ronald it could never have been accomplished. When it came to my turn to crawl from one tooth-edged rock to another along the wall, he prevented my falling into the sea with his body forming a human shield.

The boat was at last emptied and left to rise and fall in the swell of the dark green water in the grotto as we explored our unenviable position. A camp site had to be found, but where! The hole seemed to offer a good starting point and we climbed over big boulders and into its stone floor. The cliff was perhaps ten yards thick at this point and there was just sufficient space to place our tent in this wind-swept tunnel if we carefully cleared some of the larger boulders from the floor. There was no other flat spot on which we could camp. Dismally we looked at each other after examining all the possibilities. There was no alternative but to face it with good heart and fervently hope that the weather would not turn to storm conditions whilst we were marooned out at this grim spot.

The tent was raised, the ropes being fastened to solid stones that would hold it firm against the wind that kept up a steady and very irritating whine as it swept through the channel between the open sea and the slopes at the rear of the cliff face. It was cold, gloomy and bare of the slightest comfort or attraction. To make a grim situation worse, I picked up several pieces of the driftwood that littered the floor of this wind tunnel and found they were completely wet. Surely in that case they must have been washed there in the last storms of the previous week? I did not voice my fears but it was with a rather heavy heart that I eventually watched Ronald and his companion push the bows of the boat back into the light of the open sea and disappear from our sight.

We packed everything possible into the tent, leaving the water containers close by on the stones. The floor felt incredibly hard, consisting of rounded stones, and there would be little soft sleep on such a bed for the nights we should have to remain at Bryningsholm. We were now isolated, with no contact with our friends, and at the mercy of the weather. We could understand why old Monrad had been concerned about our safety.

The first evening we warmed our food over a fire of driftwood that we sheltered from the wind between a circle of stones. We needed the hot food and also hot drink, for we were bitterly cold.

It was difficult to converse at all because of the constant noise around us. The kittiwakes, never silent at any time, added their voices to the booming of the waves, for they had their nests within touching distance of the tent. There were a great many young needing to be fed and the birds did not allow our intrusion into their gloomy world to alter their routine in any way.

It was with misgivings that we crept into our sleeping-bags. The tent flapped without pause, hit by the wind blowing into the hole from the sea. Its thin canvas was all we had to protect us from anything that might happen in the night. Would the waves reach us . . . that was the question that occupied our minds as we lay listening to the sounds of this lonely wild world of the sea birds.

The night passed without mishap, however, but we were thankful to place our chilled hands round cups of hot tea in the early dawn as we prepared to face the day. We could only hope that it would not rain. The smell from our camp site made our heads ache. There was no escape from it until we came to the edge of the ragged hole and could breathe in the clear cold air. We gazed outwards with delight. It was almost as if we had discovered a Shangri La valley at the end of our gloomy tunnel.

A strong sun made the slopes seem incredibly bright after our semi-darkness. Overhead there flew so many puffins that the sky seemed completely filled with their black and white bodies and whirring short wings. Never had we imagined we should see so many birds as the vast army that flew back and forth over the tops of the great ridges in this spot.

We climbed up the first great slope in front of us. The warmth of the sun penetrated our clothing. We let it soak into our bodies, enjoying it as never before. It gave us new life and energy.

Countless holes had been bored deeply into the earth and rock slopes by the beaks of the puffins. A profusion of wild plants had gathered around the holes, for the soil had been enriched by the excrement of the birds. From deep in the earth we could hear the cheeping grunting calls of the rapidly growing young. Birds came and went in a constant rush of whirring wings and flash of crimson feet. Several puffins gathered around every hole, for there were a great many immature birds without sites of their own who appeared eager to assist in any way possible. It was good training for them. This vast array of the attractive and colourful little auks seemed to live in an ordered and peaceful colony that must be one of the largest in the north of Norway.

High over our heads, against a sky that was now very blue, the flying birds appeared as small as bees. The scene was so impressive and almost unreal that we sat bemused by it all for some time. We were roused by the sight of a pair of eagles swooping down into the heart of the flying birds between the cliffs. This caused an even greater explosive burst of noise and rushing of wings than before, as puffins in their millions hurled themselves away from the holes and down towards the sea.

Close to the slopes there were grey almost vertical rocks on which were a great many bridled guillemots and kittiwakes. These rocks did not feel the sun until late in the afternoon, and they were as coldly unappealing in the morning as the slopes were bright and gay.

The guillemots had an appeal that never diminished however long they were studied. They sat gravely all through the uproar, repeatedly bowing deeply to each other. From their ranks came deep growls that often swelled into a shouted chorus . . . 'ooorrr, ooorrrr'. The sound was unmusical but a welcome contrast to the wailing of the kittiwakes with which it blended.

The weather could not remain bright and sunny for long. Big grey clouds soon rolled in from the sea and the wind grew strong again. We were in the heart of one of the most effective natural bastions against both man and the elements that the birds could have chosen. From the heights to which we had slowly and carefully climbed we looked down on the white-tops far below. Every ledge on the cliff sides was filled . . . with kittiwakes, or massed groups of guillemots; razorbills, who preferred the very highest ridges, or parties of shags hanging out dark wings to dry in the wind.

It would have been hard to find more inhospitable surroundings for ourselves if the storms returned, for nature seemed to have designed this place entirely for the survival of these sea birds.

When the guillemots, who had been swimming in large parties out at sea all day, returned to the cliffs in the later afternoon, we were able to witness their extraordinary leaping display. In small groups they allowed the swell to bring them in right under a particular long, low and slippery rock at the base of the cliff just above the water line. As they reached it each bird gave a leap upwards, rising out of the water with a frantic flapping of black wings. In the majority of cases the first attempt was unsuccessful and the birds fell back, slipping down the smooth side of the rock as they tried to secure a hold with their big webbed feet. A second and even a third leap was necessary, but the birds persevered, and as they stood at last in a long row on the rock, flapping wings rapidly and then turning to bow to each other, the resemblance to penguins was indeed remarkable. They are of course biologically very close to the penguins of the Antarctic regions.

That night the wind rose to gale force. We were both alarmed and unable to rest at all. The fear of being swept away by the suction of a huge wave prevented any sleep.

The waves smashing against the nearby cliff face and then sweeping into our grotto until they were within a few yards of our tent were frightening in their power. The rumble and booming was magnified in our confined space, and every now and then an extra hard crash would slightly shake the floor of our tunnel.

Screaming through the big hole, the wind added to our misery. The canvas flapped madly as if it would tear apart. The ropes held, but the stones began to drag, and it was necessary to creep out of the tent and pile on more rocks and stones so that the lines were secure. We sat without speaking, mentally working out what we could do with our many pieces of equipment if the worst came to the worst. We knew that we were helpless and at the mercy of the wind and waves here, but we had to try to plan in order to keep our nerves under control.

There was only gloom and noise around us.

The hours slowly slipped by to reveal a sullen dawn and a tent covered with white spray. By a miracle for which we could never be thankful enough, the waves had stopped short of our site, although more driftwood now came to within a yard or two of the tent.

Again we made a fire as best we could, using strips of birch bark which we always carried for such an emergency. Fire in such surroundings was the most precious element over which we had any power. The orange-yellow flame, blowing fiercely in the wind, gave us fresh warmth and courage. It was too cold to think of washing and in any case we needed all the water we had for drinking.

The early morning again showed a warm and smiling face. We climbed into the sun, and using a long rope gradually edged upwards to a very narrow ledge over the big slope. From here it was possible to look directly into a deep crack in which three guillemots were covering youngsters with their warmth. Pressed close together, growling softly and constantly bowing their beautifully smooth velvety brown-black heads, the parents looked at us without fear. Their nesting ledge had a huge projecting rock above, giving them protection from the weather. At first the crack was in deep shadow, but as we watched the sun shone into the crevice, illuminating the family life with its brightness.

The head of the nearest youngster pushed out from between the wide-spread dark feet of the parent. In the manner of a small penguin it crept out into the sunlight and warmth. A charming little bird indeed, it was clothed in grey-black down on the back and wings, with the white front of the old birds. It was already a delightful miniature of the parent, who regarded it with dark eyes and head held on one side.

Flapping tiny wing stumps, the young guillemot began to preen. With swift head movements it made the fluff fly as the small beak pushed and pulled at the early down feathering. Each action was anxiously watched over by the old bird, and when the youngster strayed too close to the edge of the crack it was immediately pulled back to safety.

After some minutes the chick opened its beak wide and yawned several times. It then returned to the shelter under the left wing of the parent, who lifted the wing into just the right position to cover it completely. The small head again pushed out to survey the world from its safe and guarded warmth by the side of the female.

It was a scene of quiet contentment in marked contrast to what was to lie ahead for the still undeveloped chick when it would no longer know the security of the protecting wing. It would be pushed or encouraged by cries and growls to leave the ledge, to take its first flight into the air for which its wings were not prepared. It seems remarkable that the old birds do not wait until their youngsters are more developed, but this is not possible in the scheme of their autumn moulting, and when the late July and early August nights arrive, then they must be away.

The other two chicks were lured out by the sun and the gathering would have been most appealing had it not been for the obvious dislike each parent had for the offspring of the others. Thin dark beaks pecked viciously at the youngsters not belonging to them. The growling and irritation grew more marked when one of the males returned from a morning fishing expedition. Flying directly in from the sea, it landed on the edge of the crack, ignoring us. A small silver fish completely filled its open beak so that the tail hung over the end. The fish was swallowed quickly and with much gulping effort by the first youngster, and after a few moments gazing out to sea the male again left on another flight.

All around us the busy period of feeding the rapidly growing young of guillemot, razorbill, puffin and kittiwake continued. The month was growing to its end, and the time for a restless urge to be away would soon be here. As much food as possible must be taken from the seas during these days, for a protective layer of fat is an essential part of the growth of all the young birds in their fight to remain alive during the long autumn migrations and winter flights.

The day again grew bleak and cold after mid-morning. This was a usual pattern, and we had to accept it with resigned patience. The rocks gave us protection from the winds, and the never-silent birds made a concerto of deep growling or high wailing that mingled with the gushing whines.

The black-backed gulls were not absent from the cliffs. A sudden commotion brought our attention back to the kittiwake ledges. The whole cliff seemed to be alive with wings as they flashed around one of the big robbers flying slowly off from a ledge with a youngster hanging limply from its yellow beak. It was an occurrence that was to happen very often and was part of the nesting life.

In late afternoon, when the clouds had gathered low and coldly menacing overhead, the guillemots returned from their swimming once more. Again they made their leaps to the rocks. Despite the difficulties they had, not one of them seemed to think of flying back to land on these low rocks. All tried to leap up from the waves.

It was then that we heard the faint sound of a boat engine from the direction of Mostad. We rushed to the edge of the cliffs, but as yet we had no sight along the edge. The sound grew louder, and we broke into smiles that grew and became shouts of welcome as Ronald appeared in his small craft. He waved to us from afar, and soon the bows of the boat were gliding into the mouth of the grotto.

The packing of all our belongings was undertaken with a light heart. There was no need to stay another night in the tunnel. We should not have to remain alert and without sleep, wondering whether we should survive until the morning. The lightness of heart with which I eventually jumped down from the narrow ledge into the boat was greater than I had felt for a very long time.

Ronald had been forced to come to fetch us, he explained. Old Monrad Mickelssen had been too worried to allow us to face more nights in the danger of the tunnel. The weather forecast was bad, with the threat of gales, and we had to be picked up. It was lucky for us that the weather had been calm enough to allow us to get away from the cliff.

That night, back in the security of the school-house, the strain and coldness of the past few days began to subside . . . We could listen to the winds rising to a howling crescendo and feel the salt spray when we opened the door. The warmth of the wood fire made the small room cosy and a safe place of refuge. The old beams creaked but we could rest that night without fear.

14 *The Million Wings Depart*

The sound of steel rubbing against wet stone echoes through the empty village. Monrad is bent over a big heavy round grindstone, which he controls with one foot. The thin and very worn blades of his scythe are being sharpened for the hay cutting.

In the small fields under the precipitous cliff towering over Mostad, the grass is long and has been ready for cutting for many days. The storms have prevented all such activity, but now, in the sun and the drying wind, the old man can prepare to cut, as he has done for so many years of his long life.

The lone figure, thin as a stick, slowly cuts a path with his thin gleaming blade along the edge of the field. The grass smells rich and is still damp. The puffin hounds run around his heels, for where the old man goes so they are to be seen. As soon as he pauses, sitting for a rest on a pile of the cut grass, the dogs are around him eagerly, licking at his lined face with pleasure.

Behind his small patch of potatoes and the hay fields, on the edge of the slope that climbs so steeply up behind the village, is the old stone circular sheep pen. Later in September the sheep are rounded up, sorted in the pen, and taken back to Vaeroy by fishing boat. The lambs, that have grown so quickly and fat on the grassy slopes and the mountain tops, now weigh some 35lb, and will be worth about £8 when they are sold.

The old man bemoans the fact that the wool is not used as it once was. Formerly the women were skilful at spinning and knitting their own garments; and the patterns of North Norway are very colourful and rich in designs. But the old skills are mostly forgotten, for the younger women have not the interest in either spinning the wool or gathering the millions of vitamin-rich blueberries and cloudberries that now are thick amid the vegetation of the slopes.

The big golden-ripe cloudberries are now to be found on the top of the slopes, where footholds are scarce but the reward for the trouble and danger of gathering them is worth the effort. In the dark winter days their sweet nourishment is indeed welcome as they are easy to preserve.

Where they are most numerous the willow grouse call. The feel of autumn is in the air, despite the fact that August has only just arrived. Night after night, from ten to about midnight, we are out among the shore rocks, helping the young guillemots and razorbills to reach the sea from their tumbling falls from the nesting ledges. A feeling of restlessness is everywhere. All the millions of birds that have known this island for the summer have become infected with the same urgent desire to leave and wander over great distances in late autumn and during the winter.

The puffins are agitated and their small whirring wings seem to have little rest now. When the traditional date late in August comes and it is time for a great mass migration away from the cliffs, then the young that are not yet ready to go will be left to their fate. The young puffins are able to take care of themselves when they reach the sea, but until they do they have to contend with the slaughtering beaks of the ravens. On Vaeroy it is considered that 23 August is the date when the ravens gather in large numbers for their yearly kill.

The young puffins, deserted by their parents, remain for a short while longer in their tunnels, calling for food. When they are sufficiently hungry they emerge to stand in the light on the slopes for the first time. Their fear of the ravens, who they can hear croaking above their nesting chambers, is overcome by the need for food, and this is the moment the ravens can strike.

Just as the black-backed gulls play havoc among the young guillemots and razorbills as they struggle to reach the water, so the ravens ruthlessly kill the young puffins. Helplessly the youngsters try to escape down the slopes, but a huge number fall victim to the beaks of the glossy killers, and the eagles also swing down and take what they need. Those that reach the water are safe, being able to dive and fish and look after themselves well.

The old birds have travelled far out to sea, losing all interest in their young. They have not yet lost their ability to fly, for they do not shed their wing quills and moult until the wide open seas have been reached. There the birds are safe from predators, and the late moult, which takes place in November and December, can commence. Most of the birds even retain their old wing feathers for the whole winter, shedding the flight feathers in the spring moults of March and April when they are moving northwards to the breeding rocks once more.

The young kittiwakes have left the nesting ledges and are mingled with the old birds as they wheel restlessly around the cliff faces.

Around the school-house flutter twittering groups of delightful little redpolls, gathered in flocks and wandering slowly southwards. As Monrad gathers in his dried hay they alight on the long wires, finding plenty of seeds that have dropped from the grasses.

Over the tops of the peaks the sea eagles now soar with their two fledged young. The eaglets have not the size nor the white tail of the adults, and their flight is clumsy, but they have much to learn before the late autumn.

Along the shoreline the eiders now gather in big groups, the young being as large as the old birds and ready to start on long swimming trips with them.

The oystercatchers, who have kept in small family groups, so jealously guarding their own territories all summer, stand now in big flocks at the edge of the tide estuaries. There they remain for hours at a time, long beaks buried into back feathers as they rest, whilst those on guard trill and fly in short bursts above the main group. Suddenly, as if by common consent, the entire flock will rise and head southwards, to be seen on the island no more until next spring.

Pipits, wheatears, snow buntings, curlews, phalaropes, wagtails, all feel the urge to depart. In twittering small flocks or in pairs or even singly, they desert the slopes and the shore rocks.

The winds whine around the school-house. It is 20 August and like late autumn. It is time to write the last pages in the diary for when the storm that has raged for several days eventually blows itself out then we will have to emulate the birds and also depart.

There is now a light, yellow and solitary, shining at the end of Mostad where Monrad has his house under the towering cliff. The heights are dark and menacing in the gloom.

When the winds pass and an uneasy calm returns for a short while, we wait for the fishing boat that will take us from the village and from our isolation.

The school-house door is locked for the last time. The two young kittiwakes have not yet left their ledge by the house. They wing around us as we leave. Very soon now they will take flight for a long journey controlled by instincts about which we have little knowledge.

The old man stands on the end of his jetty, dogs by his side, waving us goodbye. The elderly couple will face another long winter with only the empty and shuttered houses to remind them of the life that the village once knew.

The ravens and the eagles will remain, patrolling along the cliffs that will be powdered with snow and devoid of the wings that gave them such generous pickings.

The air feels cold and damp . . . the summer of a million wings is over.